A People of Priests

A People of Priests

The Ministry of the Catholic Church

MICHAEL RICHARDS

Foreword by Cardinal Basil Hume

DARTON·LONGMAN+TODD

First published in 1995 by
Darton, Longman and Todd Ltd
1 Spencer Court
140–142 Wandsworth High Street
London SW18 4JJ

© 1995 Michael Richards

The right of Michael Richards to be identified as the Author of this
work has been asserted by him in accordance with the Copyright,
Designs and Patents Act 1988

ISBN 0–232–52108–5

A catalogue record for this book is available
from the British Library

The Scripture quotations in this publication are taken from *The Jeru-
salem Bible* published and copyright 1966, 1967 and 1968 by Darton,
Longman and Todd Ltd and Doubleday and Co. Inc. and the *Revised
Standard Version*, copyrighted 1971 and 1952 by the Division of Christ-
ian Education of the National Council of the Churches of Christ in the
USA.

Phototypeset by Intype, London
Printed and bound in Great Britain
at the University Press, Cambridge

TO
THE PEOPLE
OF
A PARISH
ST MARY'S,
CADOGAN STREET

Contents

Acknowledgements	ix
Foreword *by Cardinal Hume*	xi
Introduction	1
1 Christ Our Priest	17
2 Priests in Christ	46
3 Christ and the Apostles	72
4 Bishops, Presbyters and Deacons	96
5 The Priests of the Parish	118
Suggested Reading	144

Acknowledgements

I offer special thanks to Anthony Storey
for providing comprehension, critique
and encouragement at a crucial stage.

M.R.

Foreword

The Second Vatican Council's teaching on the priesthood began by reminding all Christians of their shared priesthood: but the 'essential difference' in the priesthood that the Council also declared to be conferred upon bishops, presbyters and deacons by the sacrament of Holy Orders was not then made plain and has been the subject of considerable controversy and research ever since.

The present Holy Father's preference for the word 'pastor' rather than 'pontiff' as an indication of his responsibilities, echoing his predecessor Pope John Paul I, illustrates the direction in which the meditation of the Church has been moving.

Continuing uncertainty over the character of Christian priesthood has, however, in recent years led to the resignation of a number of ordained ministers of the Church and, arguably, has given rise to a hesitation over joining the ministry.

Michael Richards has written a study of Scripture and of the Church's thought and practice that helps us to appreciate the extent of the renewal brought about by Our Lord in inaugurating the New Covenant between God and Man. An 'essentially different' kind of service is now to be offered by those chosen to call together, lead, guide and nourish his people: 'essentially different' from every kind of priesthood hitherto, but at the same time the reality that has brought the search for God in every religion and culture to its goal and completion.

FOREWORD

Only a clear vision and understanding of the mind of the Church expressed in her inspired Scriptures and in her writings and records can help us out of our present uncertainty; I believe this book provides both clarity and conviction.

ARCHBISHOP OF WESTMINSTER

Introduction

We Have a Problem

The Second Vatican Council (1962–5) laboured to equip the Catholic Church for a fresh campaign of missionary endeavour, but to many it now looks like a prelude to disaster. Even those who recognize its account of the traditional teaching of the Church as authentic and who value the changes that have been made as a result of the Council, have to acknowledge that we have not yet seen the new flowering of Christian life that it was called to promote.

The implementation of the Council has put particular strain on those most immediately affected: the parish clergy. The problem was foreseen during the Council; it was pointed out that while bishops and the laity were receiving their fair share of attention, the workers in between were being overlooked. So as to redress the balance, two documents were produced to provide for the necessary adjustment in their formation, ministry and life. But that did not prevent the onset of the hurricane. During the sixties and seventies, priests left their posts in unprecedented numbers. What the two great crises of the previous centuries – the Reformation of the sixteenth century and the French Revolution – had not done, the Church now seemed to have brought upon herself. At a time when the Church had appeared to be in secure possession of her faith, those who were supposed to be particularly dedi-

A PEOPLE OF PRIESTS

cated to commending that faith suddenly lost confidence in their calling. And in the eighties and nineties, in most countries of the world, a new generation has not so far come forward to replace them.[1]

Before the Council, the Church's understanding of her ordained ministry had appeared to be settled and assured. There had been some controversy over the worker-priest initiative, aimed at breaking down the gap between the Church and the industrial working classes, but this appeared to be a practical issue, bearing on the priest's way of earning a living and manner of life, not one involving a change in fundamental theory. But the liturgical changes brought about by the Council, altering the relationship of the priest to the people in celebrating the mass, and bringing about the translation of the Latin texts into the vernacular, represented such a transformation of attitudes and of the expectations demanded of the priest that many found themselves unable to adjust and adapt. The necessary theoretical understanding of their role, justifying and explaining the changes, was missing; all that they had was the spirituality appropriate to the doctrinal emphases of the pre-conciliar Church. Many struck

---

[1]Cf. James D. Whitehead in *Being a Priest Today*, edited by Donald J. Goergen, Collegeville, 1992: 'Priesthood in the United States has come to a crisis. The details of the distress are now familiar: a nearly 40 per cent drop in the number of diocesan priests in the last twenty-five years; the dramatic increase of priestless parishes; an evident loss of confidence among priests themselves' (p. 17). In France, 1733 priests were ordained in 1901, 1649 in 1947 and 161 in 1975 (see the graphs in the appendix to Paul Vigneron, *Histoire des Crises du Clergé Français Contemporain*, Paris, 1976). For an appreciation of the present problem as it affects the Church of England, see Anthony Russell, *The Clerical Profession*, 1980: '... the evidence for asserting that the ministry of the Church is currently undergoing a profound crisis is extensive. On the one hand there are the verifiable indices of crisis (the decline in recruitment, the increase in opting out, the high level of retirements, the aging and contraction of the profession), and, on the other hand, there are the less accessible dimensions of the crisis, of which the marginality of the profession is probably the most significant' (p. 289).

INTRODUCTION 3

out for still more of a change in the rôle assigned to them in the Church and in society; others simply refused to accept what seemed to them to be a betrayal of long-established traditions that had always been regarded as authentic expressions of Catholic faith.

The advances made in biblical studies, in history and liturgy, and the theology of the Church, had given greater credibility to the Christian faith itself, so that the time had indeed appeared ripe for a fresh examination and rethinking of the inner life of the Church and of her missionary and pastoral policy. But the translation of the results of scholarly research and of fresh thinking in response to new pastoral needs on the scale demanded by the Council has proved to be too much of a good thing. The loss of morale among the ministers of the faith, seemingly provoked by a shift in the understanding of the Church and by internal changes rather than by anti-clericals outside, has given rise to an intense campaign of self-examination in search of a reliable remedy. It has become clear that an issue that everyone would have said was settled for ever – the Church's view of her own ministry, the perennial character of the Catholic priest – is the one topic that most needs attention if the Church is to flourish in a new era of her history.

The crisis of conscience experienced by many Anglican clergy over the ordination of women has brought out still further the need for a clarification of the character of the ministry in question. On this point above all depend the further questions of who should receive ordination and by whom it must legitimately be conferred. This study does not deal directly with the question of women's ordination, concentrating on the search for an understanding of the presbyteral ministry itself by which the pastoral authority of the Church may be guided. Further remarks on this topic are to be found in Chapter 5. The significance of the theology

A PEOPLE OF PRIESTS

developed in these pages for the Catholic Church's attitude to Anglican Orders is discussed in a Postscript.

The articles and books that have been written in order to find an answer to the all too evident problems facing the present generation and to provide a firm theoretical foundation for the future work of the ordained ministry, must run into thousands, almost matching the numbers of those who have resigned from the priesthood. Sociological, psychological and historical factors have all contributed to the falling-away of the clergy and have been the object of learned attention and anxious debate. But the most pressing task is a theological one: the working-out of a generally agreed definition or job-description of the post for which recruits are sought.[2] A consensus now appears to be finding expression in a substantial part of the literature.

It must however be recognized that it has not as yet won either general recognition or authoritative acceptance. In the English edition of the *Catechism of the Catholic Church* (1994), for instance, the treatment of the Church's ordained ministry in Part One, expounding the Creed, tells us clearly that 'the Good Shepherd image ought to be the model and "form" of the bishop's pastoral office' (896), and provides substantial quotations from Vatican II on the full and equal part taken by the laity in the worship offered to God by his Church. But in Part Two, 'The Celebration of the Christian Mystery', the presentation of the ordained ministry fails to register with equal clarity the direction given by the Council to the thinking of the Church. Where the Council used 'presbyter' to bring out the special kind of priesthood that is conferred, the *Catechism* still uses 'priest' leaving the confusion between the general and the ministerial priesthood

---

[2] 'To clarify and purify the language is becoming an urgent pastoral task, because behind the language there can be traps that are much more dangerous than is generally believed', Pope John Paul II, addressing a symposium sponsored by the Vatican Congregation for the Clergy (*The Tablet*, 30 April 1994, 535).

INTRODUCTION 5

unresolved. The same failure to take in the significance of the Council's careful choice of vocabulary is to be found in two other recent documents, the Apostolic Exhortation of 1992, *Pastores Dabo Vobis* (in spite of its opening words!), and the *Directory on the Ministry and Life of Priests* published by the Congregation for the Clergy in 1994.

This book attempts to provide a statement and defence of the consensus referred to above, carrying forward previous personal attempts to reflect on this theme, published at various times since 1974 in *The Clergy Review*. It begins with an examination of a relevant passage in the documents of Vatican II, to show how the intellectual crisis began and at the same time to provide, in a study of a formal declaration made by the teaching authority of the Church, the necessary agreed basis for a fruitful discussion. It does not attempt to survey the whole history of the doctrine under debate, nor yet to give an account of all the recent thinking, but offers an examination of a theological theme which appears to provide a satisfying solution to the problem of priestly identity now facing the Church. For an Introduction, this may appear to be a rather abstruse enquiry. It is however the necessary preliminary demonstration of the contemporary shift in the Church's understanding of the ordained ministry from 'priest' to 'pastor'. Revolutionary as it may appear, this change in terminology is entirely faithful to the gospel as the Church has received it.

The difficulty experienced by those involved in the transition from the Church of the Council of Trent and the First Vatican Council to the Church envisaged by the documents of Vatican II can be illustrated from the experience of a conversation with Cardinal Heenan, Archbishop of Westminster from 1963 to 1974, who was concerned about the unfamiliar application of the title 'priest' to lay people by the Council, which had produced some confusion in both clerical and lay minds. The Cardinal explained that in order to sort

6   A PEOPLE OF PRIESTS

out the confusion he had told the Sunday congregation in the
cathedral that 'We are all priests now in the Church. But you
are little priests and I am a big priest'. As the other partner
in the conversation had been putting before the Cardinal the
point that Vatican II had rejected the reference to 'degree' –
to bigness and littleness, for example – as a way of discerning
the difference between the ordained and the non-ordained, it
seemed to him best to retire from the fray at that point in
the discussion and hope for a meeting of minds on some
other occasion.

Cardinal Heenan can help us here with a further illustration
of the difficulty experienced even by those who took part in
the Council of seeing the full significance of the wording
chosen for its decrees. The Cardinal was particularly exercised
about the quality and faithful perseverance of his clergy, and
accordingly himself undertook to translate and comment on
the decree *Presbyterorum Ordinis*, 'On the Ministry and Life
of Priests'. While the Council documents, in order to bring
out the solidarity and the necessary collaboration of bishops
and priests, had used the same words, *consecratio* and *missio*,
of the ordination of both bishops and priests, the Cardinal,
still thinking in pre-conciliar terms, retained the distinction
observed hitherto and spoke in his translation of 'consecration' and 'mission' for bishops and 'ordination' and 'function' for priests (MLP, n. 7, Catholic Truth Society, 1966. The
translation regularly uses 'priest' to translate *presbyter*). He
was not by any means alone in failing to make the necessary
adjustments of vocabulary; the confusion, as we have seen,
continues to this day in official texts.

The fundamental problem here arises out of the use of the
word 'priest' with two meanings that should be distinguished.
It derives from the Greek word *presbyteros* (Latin *presbyter*),
meaning 'elder' or 'senior person', but it now also stands for
the term *hiereus* (Latin *sacerdos*), having largely taken on the
particular reference of that word. *Hiereus* is used in Scripture

INTRODUCTION 7

for a priest of the Old Testament or else for the whole body of worshippers under the New Testament, while *presbyter* is used for an office-bearer in the New Testament Church, who is thereby distinguished from an Old Testament *hiereus* and marked out among the other members of the New Testament body of priests, the Church as a whole.

For clarification, this study will use the word 'priest' to convey the meaning of *sacerdos*, and 'presbyter' whenever that particular ordained minister is meant. In doing this, it will be following the careful attention paid to this distinction by the Second Vatican Council. The decree that began its life with the title *De Clericis*, dealing with all members of the clerical state, then became *De Sacerdotibus*, since in fact it only dealt with ordained priests; it was eventually entitled *Decretum de Presbyterorum Ministerio et Vita*, 'Decree on the Ministry and Life of Presbyters', setting aside the word *sacerdos*, so as to avoid all confusion with the priesthood (*sacerdotium*) of the faithful as a whole. The document thus made it clear that it had in mind the ordained ministers of the 'second rank', not the general body of worshippers nor, directly at any rate, the bishops of the Church.

The danger of restricting the functions of the ordained minister to the sacerdotal, cultic strand in the biblical tradition, through the application of the same word, 'priest', to the worshipping Church as a whole and to particular members of it, was thus recognized and acknowledged. To use the same word in both a general and a special sense, especially if the special sense is said to be 'essentially different', does not make for clarity. The long-standing confusion, and the inevitable restriction in practice of the rôle of the presbyter, was pointed out in the course of the elaboration of the decree, as a standard commentary on the Council has explained:

> History shows that the Church failed to overcome this danger [of confusion]. First of all we see how the sacerdotal

element in the episcopal and presbyteral offices – their cultic function – quickly became the essential and definitive element in these offices, and the other elements, especially the commission to preach, fell disproportionately into the background. . . . The Council tried to correct this line of development by refraining, even in the title, from speaking of clerics or of *sacerdotes*, and returning to the New Testament word 'presbyter'. (Friedrich Wulf in Herbert Vorgrimler (ed.), *Commentary on the Documents of Vatican II*, 1969, IV, 213).

'Presbyter' was thus deliberately used in the title and in the text of the conciliar decree to designate this particular ministry. The word has also been used in the revised rites of ordination.

Unfortunately, as we have seen, the significance of this choice of vocabulary has not always been realized, even in the translations of the decree itself, and in the work of successive Synods, down to the text of the Apostolic Exhortation *Pastores Dabo Vobis* of 1992, in spite of the emphasis given by its opening words. 'Priest' is still regularly used to translate *presbyter*, regardless of the obstacle it creates for our proper understanding. As well as telling us precisely which group of people we are talking about, the word 'presbyter' opens the way to a fresh study and comprehension of the New Testament usage, which applies the term 'priest' to Christ himself and to all the faithful without distinction, and employs the term 'presbyter' to certain members of the priestly body with special responsibility, making it clear that a new kind of religious functionary (who therefore requires a new title) has been introduced, consonant with the renewal inaugurated by Christ.

To identify the problem left to us by the Council documents, and the indication they provide of a solution, one must look at the Dogmatic Constitution on the Church,

INTRODUCTION   9

Lumen Gentium, published on 21 November 1964. The
second chapter, on 'The People of God', speaks of the
common life that is shared by all members of God's people,
who together in Christ worship and bear witness to him.
This chapter was placed before those that deal with the office-
holders in the Church, an order of exposition that puts first
what belongs equally to all, and which is therefore fundamental to any reorientation of the Church's thinking and practice.

The second section (n. 10) of this chapter runs as follows:

> Christ the Lord, high priest taken from among men (cf.
> Heb. 5:1–5), made the new people 'a kingdom of priests to
> God, his father' (Apoc. 1:6; cf. 5:9–10). . . . Therefore all the
> disciples of Christ, persevering in prayer and praising God
> (cf. Acts 2:42–7), should present themselves as a sacrifice,
> living, holy and pleasing to God (cf. Rom 12:1). They should
> everywhere on earth bear witness to Christ and give an
> answer to everyone who asks a reason for the hope of
> eternal life which is theirs (cf. 1 Pet. 3:15).

It is here affirmed, in biblical terms and with biblical references, that all the members of the People of God are priests,
and in that rôle are to worship God and give witness to him.
All share a common priesthood, given to them by Christ; all
should offer themselves as a holy sacrifice in prayer and praise
to God.

In the same section there follows a second paragraph,
couched in more technical language, and without any scriptural quotations, which is clearly designed as a commentary
eliminating any confusion that might arise from the first
paragraph's affirmation of the priestly worship offered
together, with one voice, by the whole united People of God.
Here are two current English translations of this paragraph:

> Although they differ essentially and not only in degree, the
> common priesthood of the faithful and the ministerial or

hierarchical priesthood are nonetheless ordered one to another; each in its own proper way shares in the one priesthood of Christ. (Abbott)

There is an essential difference between the faithful's priesthood in common and the priesthood of the ministry or the hierarchy, and not just a difference of degree. Nevertheless, there is an ordered relation between them; one and the other has its special way of sharing the single priesthood of Christ. (C.T.S.)

Because of the importance of this paragraph in the determination of the mind of the Council, I also give its text in the original Latin:

Sacerdotium autem commune fidelium et sacerdotium ministeriale sive hierarchicum, licet essentia, et non gradu tantum differant, ad invicem tamen ordinantur; unum enim et alterum suo peculiari modo de uno Christi sacerdotio participant.

There is, says the Council, a common, shared priesthood, exercised by all the Church of Christ; but there is another priesthood, which is not shared, and the two, quoting the Abbott translation, 'differ essentially and not only in degree' (*essentia, et non gradu tantum differant*).

This last phrase, to which the two English translations give a greater prominence than it has in the original, qualifies the otherwise straightforward affirmation of an ordered relationship between the common priesthood and the ministerial priesthood. It was clearly included to protect the self-awareness and sense of identity of the ordained priests of the Church, but it has nevertheless over the years since the Council been at the root of all the self-questioning and uncertainty that have obscured their vision and undermined their confidence. Instead of being followed by a period of fresh vigour and renewed sense of purpose among the clergy, the Council's

INTRODUCTION 11

statement has been a major factor in provoking the feeling of insecurity that has led to the resignations and the fall in recruitment. Many factors of a purely human kind are involved in the crisis, but the main one, the one to which popes, synods, bishops, theologians and commentators have constantly returned ever since the Council, is a matter of faith: priests no longer know who they are and what they do.

If there is an 'essential difference', what is it? The question has been asked repeatedly ever since, by speakers at Roman synods as well as by the ordained about to give up their ministry and return to the ranks of the laity, when they do not leave the Church altogether. In 1971 the Synod of Bishops studied the theme of the sacerdotal ministry, with a report from the International Commission to guide their reflexion. In his speech at this Synod, Cardinal Kim of Korea asked that 'the meaning of this essential difference should be made clear'. At the Synod of 1991, on the Formation of the Clergy, one still heard, twenty years on, in the words of the opening speech, that 'Many have left the ministry, while others seem to be uncertain of their priestly identity, of their faith, of their ministry' (Cardinal Simon Pimenta, Archbishop of Bombay). In his address to this Synod, Cardinal Ratzinger lamented the failure of Catholic theology to respond to the one-sided Protestant, liberal and Marxist interpretations of the ministry of Christ and his followers with a presentation that did full justice to the New Testament evidence. In the 1990s, the Decade of Evangelization, the uncertainty is still with us.

This book has been written in the conviction that the very phrase that has provoked all the anxious searching – *licet essentia et non gradu tantum differant*, 'although they differ essentially and not only in degree' – itself contains the makings of an answer to the question which is at the heart of the crisis.

Consciously or not, whoever framed that phrase opened

the way to establishing the ordained ministry on a new foot-
ing. Did he speak more wisely than he knew, or did he
knowingly offer a hint to those who would read the text in
the years that followed? It has all the marks of an insertion
deliberately added, with cautious precision, to an already
existing text. The sentence could simply have read: 'The
common priesthood of the faithful and the ministerial or
hierarchical priesthood are ordered to one another; each in
its own way shares in the one priesthood of Christ'. The
sentence would then simply have affirmed the interrelation-
ship of the two kinds of priest and their unity in the one
priesthood of Christ, and one might have thought that sufficient to stave off misunderstanding, after the earlier declaration about the common priesthood. The additional words
assert and emphasize the difference between the two priesthoods before allowing the sentence to state their relationship
and their unity. A warning is thus provided against any stress
on the unity which would lead to any doubts over the distinc-
tiveness of the 'ministerial or hierarchical' priesthood. This
in the Latin; the English translations, as we have seen, emphasize the difference still more, affirming it more definitely than
the ordered relationship.

That certainly would appear to have been the intention
behind the inserted phrase. But a careful reading shows that
while it undoubtedly rules out any assimilation of one priesthood to another, it also prepares the way for a more precise
understanding of the priesthood that it calls 'ministerial or
hierarchical'.

For it declares that this priesthood differs 'in essence' from
the common priesthood. If that is the case, then its specific
identity, that which makes it different, cannot possibly be
indicated by the common term 'priesthood'. Within the
shared priesthood of Christ, all are priests, but some are
priests in an 'essentially different' way. Clearly, that 'essential
difference', which gives its distinctive character to this par-

INTRODUCTION   13

ticular ministry, cannot be denoted by 'priesthood'; it is something else, which is not shared by all. Priesthood is held in
common, in different ways; an 'essential difference' cannot
be held in common.

The phrase we are studying provides another fundamental
clue for our search. It says that the two priesthoods differ
non gradu tantum. The originator must be given credit for
careful Latinity. He did not simply say that the difference
was 'both in essence and in degree' (*et essentia et gradu;
essentia graduque*; or, to use Vatican II's characteristic conjunction, *essentia una cum gradu*). Nor did he say that they
differ 'not only in essence but also in degree' (*non tantum
essentia sed etiam gradu*). He said that they differ 'in essence'
(and that is where his emphasis lies), and then goes on to add
'*non gradu tantum*', indicating at the very least that he was
not putting 'degree' on the same level as 'essence'. But this
particular word-order goes still further; by placing *tantum*
after the noun in this way, the writer indicates that he wants
to say 'not just in degree' 'not by a mere difference of degree',
so as to set degree aside as a way of establishing the difference.
The text is drawn up as if the writer felt that he could
not fail to mention 'degree', so familiar was it as a way of
understanding the difference, but wanted to indicate that it is
not an appropriate term.

The text thus reflects the gospel, for which 'degree' is
irrelevant and more than unhelpful. When the Apostles asked
'Who is the greatest?' (Mark 9:33–7; cf. 10:35–45), they were
given a reply that brought out the all-too-human frailty of
their question. They were firmly told to forget about degree
when it came to understanding their responsibilities and
relationships.

The decrees of the Second Vatican Council have not suf-
ficed to forestall the crisis that has fallen upon the ordained
priesthood in recent years. But they contain the elements of
renewal. We have not 'moved on' from Vatican II, any more

14   A PEOPLE OF PRIESTS

than we have 'moved on' from any of the Councils of the
Church or from the Scriptures themselves. The documents of
the Church call for the close study of their carefully worded
texts. In this case, setting 'degree' aside, we must look for
what constitutes the essence of the ordained ministry, knowing, if we are guided by the Council documents, that it will
not be 'priesthood'. To search for that essence is the purpose
of this book.

The classic character of the Council's teaching can be illustrated from the writing of an author who expressed the full
range of the Catholic faith with a wit and grace that have
given his words a permanent place in our English literary and
religious tradition. In 1951 he preached a sermon at the
Oxford Catholic Chaplaincy on the priesthood, or, to be
more precise, as he himself said, on the *presbyterate*; what
he said is a clear illustration of the teaching reaffirmed by
Vatican II.

Here are some quotations:

> ... when they were talking about a man set apart for the
> service of Almighty God under the new covenant, they
> called him a *presbuteros*, an elder ...

> The point about a *presbuteros* is exactly the same as the
> point about a senior member of the College; he is a foun-
> dation member, he belongs to the establishment.

> ... and that is still, it is well to remind ourselves, the official
> title of a Catholic priest. He calls himself *sacerdos* by a kind
> of graceful analogy; but his official title is *presbyter*.[3]

Ronald Knox never wrote as the aspiring leader of a movement or the protagonist in a controversy; but for all his
lightness of touch and adaptation to his audience, he was
clearly aware of contemporary scholarly debate. He could at

---

[3]*University and Anglican Sermons of Ronald A. Knox*, London, 1963, pp. 277–83.

INTRODUCTION   15

that time have been reading an article by Père Yves Congar
OP in a recent number of the *Revue des Sciences Religieuses*
or the same Père Congar's *Vraie et Fausse Réforme dans
l'Eglise*, first published in 1950. He was clearly aware of the
importance of the *sacerdos-presbyter* distinction, particularly
in the context of Protestant-Catholic debates, and lent the
weight of his special authority as a thinker and preacher to
what was to be a major concern of the Council: the precise
definition and understanding of the ordained ministry.

For his expression 'graceful analogy' exactly pinpoints the
theme we must explore. 'Priesthood' applies to Christ himself, to all the members of the Church, and to his ordained
ministers, but to each in a different way. Failure to discern
the modes of this analogy has led to a restricted application
of the term and a consequent distortion of pastoral practice.
When presbyters (and bishops and deacons) discover their
true place in the priestly Body of Christ, their confidence
and their energies will be restored.

This theme has so far been presented as if it were a matter
that only concerned the Catholic Church: a study arising out
of our need to clarify our thinking about the ordained ministry in order to emerge from an identity crisis. But more is at
stake than the simple survival or otherwise of a particular
religious institution. On the solution of this problem depends
the continuing presence and influence of Christianity itself.

Without the recognizable continuation in some form or
other of this 'apostolic tradition', the Christian faith would
cease to be anything other than an uplifting memory, inspiring
and perhaps worthy of imitation, but no longer possessing
the divine origin claimed for it in the first place. The authority
of Christ to speak as he did would have been dissolved
away, since he would appear to have been unable to fulfil his
promise of sending out guaranteed representatives owing
their mission in life to his choice and direction. To believe in
his living presence and influence, we need to be able to see

A PEOPLE OF PRIESTS

some continuity between the pattern of life of the New Testament community and that of the Church today. Included here is not just a recognizable structure, but the regular revision of the life of the Church under the supervision of appointed and accepted leaders.

Without such people Christianity can remain as an object of research and a source of ideas that we may if we wish make our own, but it will no longer be believed as the action of God on our behalf. If Christianity as it has been known so far throughout its history is to survive, and more than that, to revive and to continue its growth, we need to discover how its ministers represent not just the traditions and customs of a particular religious society, but the God in whose name they call that society together.

1

Christ Our Priest

Theology is the attempt made by Christ's disciples to grasp more firmly and so to obey more faithfully the Word of God made known to us in Jesus Christ. Theological development, as John Henry Newman has shown us,[1] takes place when fresh questions make us look again at the gospel we have received. The present questioning of our doctrine of priesthood is one of the periodical moments in Church history when we feel the need for further light in order to see our way forward. Our search for an answer is a search for the elimination of any partiality or inadequacy in our received understanding, so that the bearing of the original message may be recaptured, clarified and applied for the benefit of our own and future generations. Development gives us a firmer grasp on the given content of our faith through a fuller working-out of our knowledge and expression of it.

The service of the Word of God which is the continual concern of the Church is the means by which the Church grows both in extension and in maturity. Confrontation with new problems, dialogue with new partners, our own experience, including our mistakes, are all part of the process by which God teaches us, patiently allowing us to learn at our own speed. To be 'transformed by the renewing of our minds' (Rom. 12:2), we need to become aware of anything that hin-

---

[1]*Essay on the Development of Christian Doctrine* (1845).

ders that renewal: outside influences, limited responses, wrong choices that restrict our vision and lead on false trails. We must be prepared to find something different from what we already have in mind, and therefore unfamiliar; that is what readiness to learn, to be a disciple, necessarily involves. The infallibility of the Church protects us from disaster; it does not do our work for us or excuse human error when it is due to our own reluctance to learn.

The present lack of vocations may arise from the fact that we are not yet clear about what we are looking for. When things go wrong, an examination of our own theoretical understanding and its application is an indispensable part of the process of putting matters right.

The introduction to this book was largely devoted to the study of certain affirmations made in two conciliar documents that have given rise to intense controversy. This starting-point was chosen, not because theological problems can be settled simply by looking up Council texts, but because those texts represent the latest considered thinking of the appointed pastors and teachers of the Church. They are the most significant point of reference to the way in which the Church as a whole at present understands the gospel. They are our generally agreed basis for any discussion aimed at clarifying the mind of the Church. In this case, they have not solved a particular problem; they have, rather, set the terms of the problem before us. By their novelty, they have disturbed many minds and so in the short term given rise to departures and to a decline in vocations; in the long term, they provide fresh guidelines for new growth.

Knowledge of the history of the Church's teaching about priesthood will help us solve our problem provided that we realize and accept that it has been a characteristically human history of incomplete understanding, of mistakes and misleading influences as well as of essentials grasped and practised. Much of what has been said and taught has been the

CHRIST OUR PRIEST 19

unexamined repetition of what has been said before. Often enough, it is only when our attention is forcibly brought to a topic that we really begin to study it with care.

As always, we need to submit our inherited notions and the ideas we have so far acquired to the living Word of God recorded in Scripture and expressed in the life of the Church, to find the truth and the way forward. In order to see the significance of the terms used in the New Testament and in the other writings of the Church to designate priesthood and the various ways in which it is exercised, we must remind ourselves of the renewal brought about by Christ. The change in the conduct of human life of which he is the teacher and supreme example gives rise to a transformation of human institutions which is still far from being fully appreciated. Only too often, the Church lives according to the ways of unredeemed and unrestored humanity; before we look at apostles and priests, we must study the work of the One who is the Apostle and High Priest of the faith he has given us.

What Is a Priest?

A priest is a worshipper. To express his worship, he uses a variety of means, but it is not by these that he can be defined. The words and gestures he uses are manifold, but their purpose is the same: to worship, to express and foster the relationship between his own life, together with that of the community to which he belongs and for whom he acts, to the values they hold in honour and the forces by which they are governed. In these terms, there can be a public 'priestly' acknowledgement of chosen values that relates them to purely human powers; a secular state still has its worship and its official worshippers. But most commonly throughout history and throughout the world, the sacred, the holy, the absolute, the treasured standards and laws, have been above

20   A PEOPLE OF PRIESTS

and beyond humanity: they have belonged to the sphere of
the divine.

In their introduction to a recent study of pagan priesthood,[2]
the editors argue that it is difficult to arrive at a general theory
of priesthood in the ancient world. Each religion had its own
kind of official functionary; we can call them 'priests', but it
would be difficult to arrive at a common 'essence of priesthood' to be found in all cases. Just as each religion contains
elements incompatible with the special features of others, so
conceptions of priesthood will be radically different from one
another.

In particular, they say, pagan priests 'are quite unlike their
modern Christian counterparts. The priestly officials discussed in this volume bear no significant resemblance to the
comforting image of the wise Christian pastor, guiding his
flock through the spiritual perils of the world' (p. 1). Their
choice of 'pastor' as the characteristic image, replacing that
of 'priest', is, as we shall see, significant. 'Only Christianity',
they say, 'was able to define priesthood in an entirely new
way'.

That new way, expressed in a change of vocabulary, will,
one hopes, be brought out in the pages that follow. It is,
however, possible to differ at this point from Beard and North
and to maintain that while the objects of priestly worship are
extremely diverse, as are the ways in which they express their
relationship to them, there is, after all, a common element in
the activities and attitudes that we call priesthood and that
are shared by all whom we call priests. There is a continuity
as well as a break in moving from paganism to Christianity, as
in moving from the Old Testament to the New.

A priest is a worshipper. What changes is the object of

---

[2]Beard, M. and North, J. (eds.), *Pagan Priests*. Religion and power in the Ancient
World. Duckworth, 1990. See also, for the Roman world, Porte, Danielle, *Le
Donneurs de Sacré*. Le prêtre à Rome. Paris, 1989.

CHRIST OUR PRIEST 21

worship and the means used. Christian priests differ from all other priests, not because in them priesthood has been abolished, but because by being transformed it has been brought to fulfilment.

All priests relate to what is holy: all holiness comes from the God who made himself known in Jesus Christ and in doing so called together a people of priests.

The Priesthood of the Old Testament

In the ancient world in general, as among the people of the Old Testament, any individual could act as a priest on his own behalf or on behalf of others, giving thanks or making intercession to the gods. As societies became more complex, a specialized priesthood was established, allotted to particular individuals or social groups.

Both of these kinds of priesthood are to be found in the narrative of Exodus 24–31, which shows us Moses gathering together every aspect of his work for God – already, as head of the people of Israel, he acted for them as prophet, priest and king – by celebrating God's Covenant with the people, sealing their promise to obey the laws of God in worship offered at an altar built at the foot of the mountain. Others joined in, offering holocausts and communion sacrifices. It should not be thought that these ceremonies were of purely ritual significance, unrelated to the moral life of the people. Worship and obedience to the Law went together, inseparably expressed in the sacerdotal offering (Exod. 24:1–11). In the Exodus narrative, the building of the sanctuary and the installation of the specialized priesthood followed upon the celebration.

Before the creation of this special priesthood exercised by the tribe of Levi, there was therefore the general priesthood, which continued independently of it; it was exercised by heads of families, clans and tribes, and was later summed up in the priesthood associated with the royal line (Solomon, 1 Kings 8; Josiah, 2 Kings 23: 1–30), and finally with the coming Messiah, King and Priest (Ps. 110). But priesthood also became the function of a particular group. Guardians of the sanctuary, priests offered worship, interpreted the will of God through oracles, taught the law of God and gave advice over obedience to it, and offered sacrifice, expressing praise, adoration, intercession and the restoration of relationships with God that sin had broken.

The rites carried out by the priests included holocausts, in which the entire victim was consumed by fire on the altar, communion sacrifices, in which the victim was shared between God, the priest, and the persons offering the sacrifice, and expiatory sacrifices, which restored the covenant with God when it had been broken by sin. As well as animals, vegetable offerings, bread, and incense were used.

Israel did not forget that these sacrifices related to the moral demands made by the Covenant. An awareness of sin, constantly revived by the prophets, pointed to the need for a change of heart, which would be the true worship that God desired, and which was understood in a corporate as well as in an individual sense (Isa. 25; Jer. 31; Ezek. 40–48; Mal. 3:1–5). The image of the Suffering Servant in Isaiah 53 is the supreme expression of the deepest Old Testament conviction that the only acceptable expiation, offered hitherto by ritual sacrifices, would be the offering of a perfectly just and innocent life; the fact that it was offered for others was a necessary part of that perfection.

The institution of a special priesthood and the ceremonies performed by priests were already understood by the Old Testament writers to be insufficient as an expression of our relationship with God. Quite apart from the fact that priests could become corrupt, even at their best the sacrifices they offered were but external, ceremonial expressions of the auth-

CHRIST OUR PRIEST   23

entic, fully acceptable worship that was only truly offered by
personal obedience to the Law of God and the active love of
his commandments. In this the whole Law was summed up.
Without personal conformity with God's will, expressing the
justice he demands, they were worthless.

Psalm 40, echoing 1 Samuel 15:22 and later taken up by
Hebrews 10:5–7, gave expression to this:

You, who wanted no sacrifice or oblation, opened my ear,
you asked no holocaust or sacrifice for sin;
then I said, 'Here I am! I am coming!'
In the scroll of the book am I not commanded to obey your
will?
My God, I have always loved your Law
from the depths of my being. (vv. 6–8)

The sacrifices offered by the priests of the Old Testament
were material substitutes for the real thing. They reminded
those who offered them of the need for an awareness of sin,
enabling them to ask for pardon and to give thanks, but it
was the genuineness of the recognition and repentance, the
sincerity of the thanksgiving, that counted. The worship
demanded by God was a change of heart and an effective
obedience to his will, a living harmony with his creative and
loving purpose.

The prophet Jeremiah spoke of the coming of a time when
the sacrifices of the Old Testament would be replaced, when a
New Covenant would bring in the reality to which the sacrifices of the Old Law were leading: 'See, the days are coming
– it is the Lord who speaks – when I will establish a new
covenant with the house of Israel and the house of Judah. . . .
I will put my laws into their minds and write them on their
hearts' (31:31,34). The sacrifices of the Old Law and the
priesthood which went with them were God's way of preparing humanity for the complete, authentic reality to which he
was leading them: a definitive change in their hearts and

minds, bringing them into conformity with the mind and heart of God.

Along with the abrogation of the Old Law and its replacement by Christ by the New Law of the Spirit, there would be an abrogation of the old system of worship and of the priesthood that carried it out. The Old Law highlighted our failings, but did not enable us to overcome them. Similarly, the round of worship of the Temple had directed our lives towards the worship of God and at the same time had made us aware of the inadequacy of the means adopted, the sacrifices of animals and other offerings, and of our failure to correspond with the intention they expressed. These sacrifices were no substitute for genuine repentance:

> Sacrifice gives you no pleasure,
> were I to offer holocaust, you would not have it.
> My sacrifice is this broken spirit,
> you will not scorn this crushed and broken heart.
> (Ps. 51:16–17)

Truly acceptable worship was an expression of genuine obedience, real conformity in action with the words one professed. Only such practical acceptance of the Law would be recognized as authentic thanksgiving:

> 'If I were hungry, I should not tell you,
> since the world and all it holds is mine.
> Do I eat the flesh of bulls, or drink goats' blood?
> No, let thanksgiving be your sacrifice to God,
> fulfil the vows you make to the Most High;
> then you can invoke me in your troubles
> and I will rescue you, and you shall honour me.'
> (Ps. 50:12–15)

CHRIST OUR PRIEST   25

Priesthood in Roman Religion

The conflict that arose between the Church and the Empire,
between Christian worship and the pagan cults, also needs
bearing in mind if we are to discern the originality of the
Christian understanding of priesthood and sacrifice. The
Roman Empire had its many priesthoods, which were charged
with the duty of giving to the gods, in the name of the City,
the attention and the gifts that they required. Since their
beneficent approval was won, or their formidable disapproval
carefully ascertained, by the correct performance of the established ritual, the priest was charged with the most essential
of civic duties. His overriding concern was the health and
prosperity of the City.

These could only be assured by conformity with the divine
order, and since that order was unchanging, the rituals and
observances handed down from the past could never be alt-
ered. Ceremonies that bore the marks of their ancient, indeed
prehistoric origin, kept their place in public life along with
more recent observances.

To be Supreme Pontiff, the greatest of the priests, was for
the Emperor the ultimate key to personal power. He was the
one who could both keep the gods favourably disposed to
Rome and defend the Empire against her earthly enemies.

Since this identification of the interests of the divine realm
and of the political order was rejected by the priesthood as
lived out and communicated by Christ, it gave rise to the
conflict of the early centuries between the Church and
the Imperial authorities which was finally resolved by the
adoption of Christianity as the official religion of the Empire.
Pagan sacrifice was then proscribed and its priests persecuted.
But the received attitudes to ceremonial worship and to
official priesthood did not disappear overnight.

An acceptance of one degree or another of the identification
of Church and State on the Roman model, and of a pattern of

priesthood conceived on similar lines, has been a perennial temptation for the Church right down to our own times. The Second Vatican Council established fresh principles for the guidance of the Church in her relationship with political life, setting aside the 'establishment' model; the conciliar teaching on the ordained ministry similarly seeks to avoid any return to a pre-Christian view of the social function of the priest.

Christian priesthood also changed the extent of individual dedication and moral change that worship demands. In Roman religion, the relationship between humans and the gods was one of client and patron, not one of personal attachment and love. Such deeper religious needs as the desire for reassurance about one's status and survival, or the search for an escape from loneliness, were met by the mystery religions and by Christianity itself.

The sacred with which the Roman priest had to deal lay outside the realm of human life. By consecration, the priest was withdrawn from the human community. The divine domain was separate. Here again, the priesthood of Christ brought about a transformation: the Kingdom of God had entered human history, and human beings were destined to share in the divine nature. In Christ, the divine and the human were for ever united. Holiness, in Christian terms, was seen to be moral goodness, full humanity, available within life on earth. It involved abandoning the search for power or good fortune and the giving of oneself instead to the love of God and of others. Over secular and sacred, as over Church and State, the Church is involved in a perpetual struggle to grasp the bearing of the gospel and not to fall back into accepting notions that belong to times when we were ignorant of Christ.

CHRIST OUR PRIEST

Christ the Priest of the New Covenant

'The hour is coming, and now is, when the true worshippers will worship the Father in spirit and truth' (John 4:23). Speaking to the Samaritan woman, Christ explicitly declared that the time of preparation, the time of shadows, had come to an end; he had been sent to establish the authentic way of worship for all humanity. In other words, he was inaugurating a new kind of priesthood, one which would express in real terms, in figure no longer, the relationship between God and his creation, and which would therefore make priesthood available to everyone.

The author of the Epistle to the Hebrews explained in detail the way in which the work of Christ had achieved this end. The ceremonies and the priesthood of the Old Law had reminded us of our deficiencies, but they did not themselves constitute the worship desired by God: '. . . in these sacrifices there is a reminder of sin year after year. For it is impossible that the blood of bulls and goats should take away sins' (10:3–4). Instead, we now have the offering of a created human life lived throughout in authentic, complete and loving harmony with the life of the Creator. Christ was the one human being who had lived on earth the kind of life that the prophets and writers of the Old Testament had constantly taught and urged upon the people of Israel. Christ was qualified to be our 'priest, not according to a legal requirement concerning bodily descent, but by the power of an indestructible life' (7:16). Throughout this 'indestructible life', he had shown himself to be set apart by the Spirit of God 'to bring good news to the poor' (Luke 4:18), as he declared at the outset of his mission. And that he had done by his preaching and by deeds that confirmed his words. He had never turned aside from the pattern of life and the purpose that he was called upon to carry out.

In all of this, he was acting as the true worshipper of his

heavenly Father, offering thanks to God for all his providential care and his special blessings, and constantly acknowledging the source of all goodness: 'At that time Jesus exclaimed, "I bless you, Father, Lord of heaven and of earth, for hiding these things from the learned and the clever and revealing them to mere children. Yes, Father, for that is what it pleased you to do" ' (Matt. 11:25). Sincere thanksgiving, backed up by a life saved in profound conformity with the Law of God and that kept all its promises to serve him: this was the way to establish friendship with God and deserve his answer to our prayers in our everyday difficulties. God was honoured by a human life consciously lived in harmony with his purpose, reflecting his own love for us, his giving of himself for our happiness.

Christ did not simply teach about worship; he was in his very being a perfect example of what worship is. Every detail of his life was lived in love and obedience towards his heavenly Father, and in love and service towards the men and women he came to save. The way of worship he had come to make possible for us he himself embodied in his life among us.

Here was a man living in the world, involved in every aspect of daily life in the society into which he was born, who acted in every way as the Law and the Temple were meant to bring people to act.

It was his blameless life, a constant victory over sin which was finally demonstrated overwhelmingly by the Resurrection, that gave the author of the Epistle the heart of his argument.

His life: this was Our Lord's only claim to being acknowledged by those who had seen and heard him as God's true worshipper. And it was the essential one. He was not a priest in the official sense. He did not come from the tribe of Levi, from the priestly caste descending from Aaron that was the living embodiment of the worship of the Old Testament.

CHRIST OUR PRIEST 29

Their worship 'can never take away sins' (Heb. 10:11).
'. . . The one of whom these things are spoken belonged to
another tribe, from which no one has ever served at the altar.
For it is evident that Our Lord was descended from Judah,
and in connection with that tribe Moses said nothing about
priests' (Heb. 7:13–14). That Christ was not a priest in the
tribal or ceremonial sense – that he was not a Temple official
– could not be said more clearly. He is a priest for us because,
differing in this from the Old Testament priests, he had
achieved everything towards which their priesthood was
pointing. He is called our priest in virtue of the life he lived,
not in virtue of physical descent from a particular tribe or of
participation in public ritual. 'During his life on earth, he
offered up prayer and entreaty, aloud and in silent tears, to
the one who had the power to save him out of death, and he
submitted so humbly that his prayer was heard' (Heb. 5:7).

To bring this out further, the Epistle calls him a priest
'according to the order of Melchizedek', since Melchizedek
was a king 'of justice and peace' whose blessing was acknowledged by Abraham and who came upon the scene (Gen. 14)
as a solitary figure from outside Israel 'without father or
mother or genealogy', and who 'has neither beginning of days
nor end of life' (Heb. 7:3). The worship offered by Christ,
like that offered by Melchizedek and acknowledged as authentic by Abraham, was not a simple extension of the worship
offered by the tribe of Levi, but was a radically new departure. The fulfilment of the Old Law, in justice and peace, was
also a new beginning.

Melchizedek symbolized the fact that Christ fulfilled the
Law by living a just and peaceful life among God's people
and for the building up of God's people. Because he offered
himself without blemish to God, his was the perfect sacrifice
that the blood of goats and bulls could never be (Heb.
9:11–14).

You who wanted no sacrifice or oblation, prepared a body
for me.
You took no pleasure in holocausts or sacrifices for sin:
then I said,
just as I was commanded in the scroll of the book,
'God, here I am! I am coming to obey your will.'
(Heb. 10:5–7, quoting Ps. 40:7–9)

Not a ceremonial worshipper, but a real worshipper: Christ
was an ordinary member of the house of Judah who in his
daily life and work had carried out perfectly the will of
his heavenly Father.

The Life of Christ: Worship Offered in Obedience and Love

The arguments and the message of the Epistle to the Hebrews
were based on the evidence of Christ's life. Already, as a
child, he had said that this perfect obedience was the purpose
of his life (Luke 2:49). The episode of the Finding in the
Temple (Luke 2:41–50) marked the beginning of his achievement. He set aside the authority of his parents in favour of 'his
Father's business'; he was clearly the bringer-in of something
fresh and new, for the doctors of the Law with whom he
conversed 'were astounded at his intelligence and his replies'.
In the context of the Temple and its worship, he indicated
that obedience to the Father must take precedence over family
duty and man-made laws.

At his baptism, the promised Spirit, who was to come so
as to enable the Law to be perfectly carried out, descended
upon him, and the Father declared that his worship was
acceptable (Luke 3:21–2).

The Temptations in the Desert, which Jesus confronted
'filled with the Holy Spirit', all tested his will and capacity

CHRIST OUR PRIEST 31

to offer true worship as it was understood in the writings of
the Old Testament: they challenged his purpose as the one
who would fulfil all priesthood.

The temptation of hunger was resisted by the strength of
his conviction that 'Man does not live on bread alone' (Luke
4:4). The reference is to Deuteronomy 8:3; human beings
were not to live on food for their bodies, but 'on everything
that comes from the mouth of the Lord'. God's words were
life-giving; his commandments sustained humankind.
Through obedience to the creative words of God, our lives
are continually nourished. Christ himself sought nourishment
for his life in his obedience to the Law, as St John's Gospel
makes plain: 'My food is to do the will of the one who sent
me, and to complete his work' (John 4:34).

The temptation to presume on God's merciful care by
throwing himself down from the parapet of the Temple strikes
at the heart of sincere worship, which does not seek to use
God for our own personal ends, as if his power were at our
command. He rejects it: 'You must not put the Lord your
God to the test' (Luke 4:12 and Deut. 6:16).

The temptation to worship the devil rather than God and
to receive the kingdoms of this world as a reward threatened
the very basis of his life of obedience to the Father. His reply
is his constant affirmation from the beginning to the end of
his life: 'You must worship the Lord your God, and serve
him alone' (Luke 4:8 and Deut. 6:13).

The true priest is called to live in complete dependence on
the will and purpose of God. Worship is not a way of winning
personal benefits, but the simple acknowledgement of God's
purpose and the desire to accomplish it. And by making his
priestly offering of perfect worship to the Father, Christ also
brought to completion the work of preparation carried out
before him by prophets and kings.

The very next episode recorded in St Luke's Gospel shows

Jesus presenting himself as the one who answers to Isaiah's portrait of the prophet:

> The spirit of the Lord has been given to me,
> for he has anointed me.
> He has sent me to bring the good news to the poor;
> to proclaim liberty to captives
> and to the blind new sight,
> to set the downtrodden free
> to proclaim the Lord's year of favour.
> (Luke 4:18–19, quoting Isa. 61:1–2)

In this declaration of his purpose, he spoke as an ordinary member of the Nazareth synagogue and he used Isaiah's text to point to himself as one called to restore justice in human affairs: to release all who suffered from the oppression of the rich or of their rulers, from physical suffering or ignorance and from the burden of sin. All of these were real tasks to be accomplished in the public domain. And the fulfilment was to be seen in his own life.

Just as he was not a priest or a scribe as Israel knew priests and scribes, so also, to apply to him his own words about John the Baptist (Matt. 11:9), he was 'much more than a prophet': he was in himself and in his actions the embodiment of the public and private life desired by God as true service and worship. Nor was he a king exercising earthly rule; rather, he came to rescue humanity from exploitation by their rulers and to be their ruler himself in quite a different way.

He achieved in a human life which was without any official social function the purpose which those functions had, in the Old Testament, been established to bring about. Through it all, he persevered against the opposition of those who refused to recognize him as an authentic representative of all that their faith stood for.

His 'ordinariness' meant that not only was he devoid of any public office, but that he could not be identified with any

CHRIST OUR PRIEST

of the parties into which the Jewish people and religion were divided. He was not a Pharisee or a Sadducee, a Zealot or a Herodian. At one with the inner spirit and purpose of the Law, he was not marked out either as one who collaborated with the ruling powers, the Romans, or as one who violently rejected them, either as a conservative in religious matters or as a reformer wanting to adapt to contemporary culture. His claim to bring the Law to completion, both in his teachings and in his daily life, could not be faulted. He did not seek to define himself by taking up any special cause or sectional interest, except that of the poor, who had no place in society. He associated with the tax collectors and sinners whom respectable society – the Pharisees and the scribes – looked on as beyond the pale.

His teaching about the true worship desired by God, which went above and beyond the worship of the Temple, was shown in the episode of the breaking of the Sabbath by his disciples, who picked and ate ears of corn on a walk through the cornfields. To defend their action, he quoted the example of David and his followers who ate the loaves offered in the Temple. 'Now here, I tell you, is something greater than the Temple. And if you had understood the meaning of the words *What I want is mercy, not sacrifice*, you would not have condemned the blameless. For the Son of Man is master of the Sabbath' (Matt. 12:7). His words apply to himself; he would die because the authorities refused to recognize the nature of the worship he offered. To show the significance of what was an acted parable, he invoked the principle of which Old Testament writers were already aware (Hos. 6:6).

He did not write off the external and formal expression of worship as useless – he taught in the synagogue and the Temple – but he insisted that only sincere prayers drawn from a sound and genuine source are acceptable to God: 'A good man draws what is good from the store of goodness in his heart' (Luke 6:45). One must 'listen to his words and act

34 A PEOPLE OF PRIESTS

on them' (Luke 6:47). He constantly leaves us in no doubt
that the truth of worship is tested by our inner attitudes and
motives and by our real actions. When he wanted to pray, he
went away to a lonely place; and he advises us to do the
same, so that our reward may be hidden, and not something
from which we hope to gain kudos and personal advantage.

Christ's teaching about worship shows us what kind of
priesthood he had in mind. He demanded real conformity
with the Law of God and criticized those who identified
worship with the correct performance of ritual. When the
Pharisees and scribes accused his followers of not observing
the tradition of the elders over ceremonial washing, he
attacked them as hypocrites, quoting the prophet Isaiah:

> This people honours me only with lip-service,
> while their hearts are far from me.
> The worship they offer me is worthless,
> the doctrines they teach are only human regulations.
> (Mark 7:6; Isa. 29:13)

Hypocrites found ingenious ways of getting round the moral
demands of God's Law (Mark 7:8–13). But the true disciple
was one 'who does the will of my Father in heaven' (Matt.
7:21; Luke 6:46), and whose conduct would bear scrutiny in
secret. For prayer was best offered in private (Matt. 6:5,6).
Outward gestures could have many different meanings and
motivations; those who welcomed the Word of God in their
hearts (Heb. 4:12–13) could be certain that their worship
would be received. 'Your Father who sees all that is done in
secret will reward you' (Matt. 6:6).

Such is the perverse ingenuity of the human mind that even
this teaching about inner worship can be twisted and turned
into an excuse for avoiding public commitment. But Our
Lord made it clear that we cannot escape so easily. To be a
follower of the Kingdom means public identification with
himself and his cause. There were those who found his teach-

CHRIST OUR PRIEST

ing too much for them and turned aside. Those who continued to be with him remained because they knew they were hearing 'the words of eternal life' (John 6:67–9). Their worship, their obedience, motivated by personal faith, was public and obvious to all. Public worship, the welcome given to him as Messiah on his entry to Jerusalem, was genuine and sincere; those who refused their hosannas were those whom he had previously denounced for hypocrisy.

One must not underrate the force of Our Lord's words condemning the Temple worship of his own day and the hypocrisy of the Pharisaic interpretations of the Law. Matthew 23 stands as a devastating indictment of the compromises and crimes that had offended against the justice that God demanded: ' "You who pay your tithes of mint and dill and cummin and have neglected the weightier matters of the law – justice, mercy, good faith!" ' (v. 23) Unless he were bringing in a higher standard and making it possible for men and women to attain it, his words would themselves be examples of self-righteous hypocrisy. He made it absolutely clear that he did make those claims, that true holiness is justice, mercy and sincerity in the dealings of everyday life, and that he would send his representatives to establish the new regime, his own 'prophets and wise men and scribes', not Temple officials (Matt. 23:34). They, too, would not be universally welcomed: 'Therefore I send you prophets and wise men and scribes, some of whom you will kill and crucify, and some you will scourge in your synagogues and persecute from town to town, that upon you may come all the righteous blood shed on earth' (Matt. 23:34–5).[1]

---

[1]His words will be remembered in the Church: 'Realize that here below, since the beginning of the world, justice has had to undergo a severe struggle in every age. Right in the beginning, the just Abel was killed, and from then on all the just men and the prophets and apostles have received their mission' (St Cyprian, martyred bishop of Carthage in the third century, Letter 6, 1–2; a reading from the Common of Martyrs).

36   A PEOPLE OF PRIESTS

The Temple would be destroyed, to be replaced by the
Temple of his Body, the Church. There Christ's warnings are
still read and still stand. Membership of his Body entails the
justice in all our dealings that he practised and demands of
us; and finally we will be judged not on outward membership,
not even on conscious membership, but on whether, knowingly or not, we have lived according to the justice he taught
from the outset of his mission and finally summed up in his
account of the Last Judgement. Many who did not recognize
him in those whom they helped, observing the laws of justice
without knowing to whom they had to answer, will be
received into his kingdom. Having been true priests in this
world, they will continue to worship him in the next (Matt.
25:31–46).

A Priest for the People

Jesus was concerned for the mass of the people, and taught
and performed his miracles among them; his concern was
recognized. 'The people as a whole hung on his words' (Luke
19:48). For all its informality, the service he offered to his
heavenly Father was public worship. It meant something to
the people, and it did something to the people. It was completely without ceremony, in the sense that one cannot at
any moment detect in his words and actions an outward
performance of prescribed gestures without full interior conformity with what was expressed. The reality of his interior
attitude was seen by others and called forth their response.
His personal worship took on a corporate character; other
people were drawn in, manifesting by their reactions their
sympathy with what they saw and heard, and their assent to
it, and so joined in his worship.

In that way, he became their priest. He led their worship of
the Father by what he told them to do, by the example he

CHRIST OUR PRIEST   37

gave, and by the atmosphere he created. The last words of St
Luke's Gospel sum up the impression he left on them and
the response of true disciples. After the Ascension, 'They
worshipped him and then went back to Jerusalem full of joy;
and they were continually in the Temple praising God' (Luke
24:51–3). In Christ, the purpose of the Temple had been
achieved.

The Prayer of Christ: John 17

Chapter 17 of St John's Gospel has come to be known as
Christ's priestly prayer. And yet priesthood is not expressly
mentioned in it. Its commonly used title must not mislead us
by allowing us to stop short of its full meaning. John's text
shows us how Christ has gone beyond priesthood in the Old
Testament or pagan sense to live the reality towards which
pre-Christian priesthood was leading us. He is not taking on
the role of a priest as the Old Testament understood it; in his
whole self, he is living the life which sums up and transcends
all other priesthoods. He is looking forward to the new pattern of life that he has brought into the world, and so he
speaks of apostolate rather than priesthood. He speaks of
having been sent into the world to make God's name known,
and he prays for the Apostles, who are going to be sent into
the world in their turn. The whole thrust of the prayer would
be better summed up if it were called the apostolic, rather
than the priestly, prayer of Christ, so as to indicate precisely
the way in which he and his disciples give glory to God.

In his prayer to the Father, Christ speaks of his mission
and gives direct expression to his own personal life. He had
promised his disciples that 'the hour is coming when I shall
no longer speak to you in metaphors, but tell you about the
Father in plain words' (John 16:25). And here he does speak
'in plain words'. He avoids the technical expressions that

were used for the preparatory phase of worship under the Old Covenant, and himself utters the true worship that he has been sent to offer and to make possible for others. He does more than talk about it or explain it; he makes it known by living it, no longer speaking in images and comparisons.

Priesthood can be seen as one of the metaphors through which God's meaning has been conveyed; the reality is something more and something other, and in John 17 we glimpse that reality, not spoken about, but speaking. The relationship of Father and Son is revealed as it is lived.

Our Lord does not speak here of the mission he had come to carry out as if it were a task added to his fundamental existence; it is his life itself, a single perfect act of loving obedience, a life of worship.

The 'broken spirit' of the Psalmist acknowledges its sin, recognizing its true self and at the same time its duty to God. Christ, without sin, acknowledges the will of the Father; the 'brokenness' of his spirit is due to our sin, for he loves us and in compassion seeks to save us.

Speaking to his heavenly Father, he expresses the fact that his capacity for worship, his ability to 'glorify' the Father, comes in the first place from the Father himself. Worship is the acknowledgement of dependence on a giver, of the source from which everything comes: this as true of the uncreated Godhead as it is of created human beings. And it is by being the Son that he will glorify the Father: not by a role that he might have taken on, such as that of prophet or priest, but by his very being itself, by his Sonship. The praise given to God the Father on earth had existed from all eternity; it had been the same from the very beginning (17:5).

'Being the Son' on earth involved giving eternal life to all those destined to receive it. And eternal life is here defined as knowledge:

CHRIST OUR PRIEST

'... eternal life is this:
to know you,
the only true God,
and Jesus Christ whom you have sent.' (17:3)

Just as the function (priest) was identical with the person (the Son), so the knowledge given was identical with the eternal life of God. It was not knowledge about God, or of the way to find him, but shared direct knowledge of him as he is in himself.

The communication of this knowledge, it is here made abundantly clear, is the work that Christ was sent into the world to do, and that he shared with his Apostles:

'I have made your name known to the men you took from the world to give me.' (17:6)

'... Now at last they know that all you have given me comes indeed from you.' (17:7)

'... I have given them the teaching you gave to me.' (17:8)

'... I passed your word on to them.' (17:14)

'... Consecrate them in the truth; your word is truth.' (17:17)

'... for their sake I consecrate myself so that they too may be consecrated in truth.' (17:19)

'... Father, Righteous One, the world has not known you, but I have known you, and these have known that you have sent me.' (17:25)

'... I have made your name known to them, and will continue to make it known.' (17:26).

It is through knowledge that people are to be made capable of sharing in the perfect worship offered by Christ to the Father: knowledge that Christ was sent into the world to communicate, as the Apostles were now to be sent. They were to be consecrated 'in truth'; their holiness would be a knowing and willing obedience to their mission, which continued that of Christ: 'As you sent me into the world, I have sent them into the world' (17:18). Worshipping the Father means, for Christ, associating others with his own action. His duty is to look after those who had been entrusted to him (17:6) – 'for their sake I consecrate myself' (17:19) – and that duty had been accomplished. His holiness was a shared holiness. Without that corporate dimension, it would not have been complete.

And the sharing went beyond the Apostles, to those to whom they would speak: 'I pray not only for these, but for those also who through their words will believe in me' (17:20). God's gifts are not given for the private benefit of the individual, but to enrol him in the service of others according to God's purpose. If glory was given to the Son, because he has won eternal life for others, those whom he calls to share his mission will be rewarded in the same way for their dedication, not to their own self-improvement, but to the salvation of others, whose company they will always desire:

'I want those you have given me
to be with me where I am.' (17:24)

'I have made your name known to them
and will continue to make it known,
so that the love with which you loved me may be in them,
and so that I may be in them.' (17:26)

For Christ, worship necessarily included sharing his worship, so that they could worship with him.

CHRIST OUR PRIEST

'It Is Finished'

Reflection on the priesthood of Christ has always concentrated on the last moments of his life: his passion, death and resurrection. In those days of crisis his character was tested and revealed to the full. Without that confirmation of his teaching about death to self, he would have been a giver of good advice, but not necessarily the supreme practitioner, the definitive example. By completing his own programme to the end, he became the one who enables and empowers us to do the same. Once the victory over sin and death had been accomplished by one member of the human race, the way was open for others to follow him. Since his whole life was for others, in loving obedience to his heavenly Father, the fruits of his victory were for us as well. They are given to us so that our own victory is made possible.

It is in this sense that Christ's death on the Cross is properly called a sacrifice. Human sacrifice had been set aside long ago as an appropriate way of expressing our relationship with God. The story of the sacrifice of Isaac as Abraham proposed it and its replacement by the sacrifice of a ram made that clear (Gen. 22). Abraham's willingness to give his son as an offering to God had demonstrated his fear of God, his readiness to obey: that was enough.

So the death of Christ cannot be reduced to the level of the proposed death of Isaac or to the various forms of ritual sacrifice that replaced it and expressed Israel's worship of God, atonement for sin and restoration of communion. His life and death attained in reality the aim towards which ceremonies of that kind were pointing; the offering of a living, not a dead, person made whole and holy through daily cooperation with the grace of God. The Cross revealed the extent of humanity's rejection of God; in accepting it Christ revealed the persevering consistency of God's love for humanity.

St Augustine taught that 'everything we do that brings

about our union with God in holy fellowship is a true sacrifice' (*Verum sacrificium est omne opus quo agitur ut sancta societate inhaeremus Deo (De Civitate Dei, X,6)*). To sacrifice, *sacrum facere*, is, literally, to make holy. To sacrifice is to separate from sin, to give oneself to the work of justice and the love of God, and to receive, to take in, a transformation and a union with the holiness of God. To be separated, we need his grace; to be just, we need his grace; and to be one with him, we need his grace. Because Christ is the priest whose worship of God has made available this new life for us, we can now be priests in our turn, offering human lives wholly transformed from within by the communication of his life.

Christ's life on earth was so filled with the Spirit of God – the holiness of God – that in its completeness from birth to death it was that perfect offering, that perfect communion with God, that is the fulfilment of a human life. If he had turned aside from the Cross his life would have been a failure, for he would have gone back on his words. His holiness was a complete giving of himself to us in order that we might be won back to God. That holiness was from first to last entirely for our needs; the resurrection confirmed the accomplishment of his purpose. He did not simply deliver a message, back it up by his example, and then disappear from the scene. He has assured his disciples that the victory over sin and death has been completely won, and after returning to Heaven he has sent his Holy Spirit to witness to him in our hearts. His concern for us has never ceased.

'The Apostle and High Priest of our Religion'

The Epistle to the Hebrews situates this life of perfect worship offered by Christ on earth to his Heavenly Father within the context of the worship now offered by members

CHRIST OUR PRIEST

of his Church and of the heavenly worship of which this is a part: 'Christ is the apostle and High Priest of our religion' (Heb. 3:1).

It was by being an apostle – carrying out the work for which he was sent – that Christ was a priest, a worshipper. It is significant that his apostleship is mentioned first, as the category within which his work is to be understood, and as the category, therefore, within which the continuation of his work through his disciples is to be understood.

Worship and its characteristic emotions are part of that continuation: 'The disciples were filled with joy when they saw the Lord, and he said to them again, "Peace be with you. As the Father sent me, so am I sending you" ' (John 20:21). As the Apostle of God, he was sent to enable us to give true worship to God, and part of the work of enabling us to give this worship, in shared obedience to the Father, was his choice and sending out of the disciples as apostles in their turn. They were to do what he himself did – be apostles – so as to give glory to the Father.

This obedience to his apostolic mission was his priesthood. He was faithful to that mission as son and as master of the house, the house that we are, being built up by his work for us (Heb. 3:5–6). 'He submitted so humbly that his prayer was heard' (Heb. 5:7); 'having been made perfect, he became for all who obey him the source of eternal salvation' (Heb. 5:9). His priesthood of perfect obedience can make us into priests, with a priesthood totally present to the world as we know it, practising real justice and rejecting human selfishness in the service of the weak.

It is a priesthood that he exercises now both in heaven and on earth. In heaven, in eternity, his work has reached completion, which means, not that he has abandoned it, put it aside, but that he is fully alive and active in his worshipping love of the Father, which includes his love of us and his prayer for us. On earth, in time, through the provision that he made and through his own presence, his work continues: his teaching, safeguarded by his Church, and the signs through which our salvation is expressed and conveyed. Making our worship acceptable, he gathers us together, so that with him we may offer our lives in thanksgiving to God.

The Holiness of Christ and of Christians

Priests deal with holiness. Different ideas of what constitutes holiness give rise to different ideas of priesthood. Places, times, people: all of these can be holy. How do we 'situate' Christian holiness?

'The Lord is in his holy Temple: let the whole earth be silent before him' (Hab. 2:20). The prophet Habakkuk declares that this holiness of God makes moral demands upon humanity, requiring recognition, respect and obedience on earth. Present among us in his Temple, the Lord challenges and overthrows injustice, exploitation, the plundering and destruction of nations, debauchery, trust in empty idols.

> Trouble is coming to the man
> who amasses goods that are not his, ...
> who grossly exploits others, ...
> who builds a town with blood,
> and founds a city on crime, ...
> who makes his neighbours drink,
> who pours his poison until they are drunk, ...
> who says to the piece of wood, 'Wake up!'
> to the dumb stone, 'On your feet!'
> (Hab. 2:6, 9, 12, 15, 19)

In his teaching on holiness, Christ denounced the crimes of humanity with even greater directness and force (Matt. 23). 'You must be perfect just as your heavenly Father is perfect' (Matt. 5:48). Christ taught that human holiness must

CHRIST OUR PRIEST

be like the holiness of God himself: a giving without reserve, a love which has no favourites. So the holiness we look for is the holiness of God. In this world, it will be found in other people who live by that holiness. Holiness is both a superhuman quality and a human quality. It is not a sub-human, blind force, a neutral or negative power.

Holiness can be described in human terms: the terms used in the Sermon on the Mount, or in the list of gifts of the Spirit given by St Paul (Gal. 5:22–3).

Because the power of holiness is felt and because it challenges us to change, painfully because we do not want to give ourselves to others, it meets with resistance. It is not because Christ was weak that he was persecuted and tortured to death, but because he was strong. His strength, the truth of his teaching and the power of his conviction, was too much for his opponents. They had either to give in and become his disciples – the way of strength, overcoming self and sin – or they had to wipe him out – the way of the coward, who refused to listen, to understand and to grow.

The holiness of Christ is the service of the weak, but it is more than that; it is above all the service of the Holy One, and therefore condemnation of the strong who are unjust to the weak and who refuse to obey God.

That is why the priesthood of his followers will be as much hated by some as it will be loved by others. Christ's holiness is real and can be recognized; to recognize and acknowledge is already to share. It does not alienate us from everyday life. It is not a way of escape, an evasion of responsibility. At the end, it will not be assessed by our churchgoing, but by the extent to which that churchgoing changed our lives.

2

Priests in Christ

For centuries, Catholics have been accustomed to calling ordained ministers 'priests' and have not used the term of the other members of the Church. In order to stress the priesthood of the laity, Protestants have done the opposite, avoiding the term 'priest' for their ministers.

Before the Second Vatican Council, Catholic attempts to do justice to the priestly character of the whole Church treated the priesthood of the laity as a participation in the prior priesthood of the clergy; the apostolate was thought of in a similar way.

The Council documents corrected this presentation, beginning by recalling the priestly character of all Christians. Under the New Testament, all are priests, all are empowered to offer acceptable worship to God in their daily life and work. As we have seen, this has led to some confusion among the ordained, in spite of the Council's reminder about the 'essential difference'. For them, priesthood was that difference; the non-ordained were not priests.

This chapter attempts to set out the New Testament understanding of the priesthood that we all share and that never ceases to be a common denominator for all members of the Church.

PRIESTS IN CHRIST 47

'The Right to Enter the Sanctuary'

Three New Testament passages affirm with particular clarity the fact that Christ's fulfilment of all priesthood through his life of perfect obedience has opened the way for us all to be priests, offering the kind of worship that is acceptable to Almighty God.

In John's vision, the elders (*presbuteroi*) expressed this in the hymn they sang in honour of the Lamb:

> 'You are worthy to take the scroll
> and break the seals of it,
> because you were sacrificed, and with your blood
> you bought men for God of every race,
> language, people and nation
> and *made them a line of kings and priests,*
> *to serve our God and to rule the world*'. (Rev. 5:9–10)

The first Epistle of Peter speaks in the same way of a priesthood that has come into being as a result of Christ's work:

> He is the living stone, rejected by men, but chosen by God and precious to him; set yourselves close to him so that you too, *the holy priesthood that offers the spiritual sacrifices which Jesus Christ has made acceptable to God*, may be living stones making a spiritual house. (1 Pet. 2:4–5)

> But you are a chosen race, *a royal priesthood*, a consecrated nation, a people set apart to sing the praises of God... (1 Pet. 2:9, my italics)

And without using the words 'priest' or 'priesthood', the Epistle to the Hebrews evokes the life of the Church in which everyone can now act as a true worshipper, and so as a true priest of the New Testament:

> ... what you have come to is Mount Zion and the city of the living God, the heavenly Jerusalem where the millions

48 A PEOPLE OF PRIESTS

of angels have gathered for the festival, with *the whole Church in which everyone is a 'first-born son' and a citizen of heaven*.

We have been given possession of an unshakeable kingdom. Let us therefore *hold on to the grace that we have been given and use it to worship God in the way he finds acceptable*, in reverence and fear. (Heb. 12:22–3, 28, my italics)

These texts declare that the kind of life in harmony with God and in community with others that had been foretold by the prophets was now in their own time present and available within human society. In the Church, everyone shared the same citizenship, stemming from the same birth. The grace that they had been given enabled them to act as priests: all were capable of offering true worship.

In the seventh century BC, Jeremiah had spoken of the New Covenant that God was preparing. In the New Israel, everyone would have direct access to God, in virtue of their changed hearts, now brought into harmony with his Law.

See, the days are coming – it is the Lord who speaks – when I will make a new covenant with the House of Israel ... Deep within them I will plant my Law, writing it on their hearts. Then I will be their God and they shall be my people. There will be no further need for neighbour to try to teach neighbour, or brother to say to brother, 'Learn to know the Lord!' No, they will all know me, the least no less than the greatest – it is the Lord who speaks – since I will forgive their iniquity and never call their sin to mind. (Jer. 31:31, 33–4)

At the time of the Exile, in 592 BC, Ezekiel's vision of the restored House of Israel affirmed the same renewal:

I will give them a single heart and I will put a new spirit in them. I will remove the heart of stone from their bodies

PRIESTS IN CHRIST   49

and give them a heart of flesh instead, so that they will keep
my laws and respect my observances and put them into
practice. Then they shall be my people and I will be their
God. (Ezek. 11:18–20)

The People of God will be given not just the knowledge of
the Law of the gospel, but the power to obey it: not just a
new organization, a revised constitution, but a renewal from
within. Each one of them without distinction will be able to
offer true and acceptable worship. The words of Jeremiah
and Ezekiel reaffirm and strengthen the classic assurances
given in the Book of Deuteronomy: 'For this Law that I
enjoin on you today is not beyond your strength or beyond
your reach.... No, the Word is very near to you, it
is in your mouth and in your heart for your observance'
(Deut. 30:11, 14). The prophetic expectation gives depth and
strength to the New Testament conviction. With the coming
of Christ, there was made possible a real interior renewal, a
change in people's hearts: genuine worship, available to each
individual. 'There will be no further need for neighbour to
try to teach neighbour... No, they will all know me'
(Jer. 31:33–4).

   The fulfilment of this prophecy was explicitly affirmed by
Christ:

> It is written in the prophets:
> They will all be taught by God,
> and to hear the teaching of the Father
> and learn from it,
> is to come to me. (John 6:45)[1]

---

[1]The Second Vatican Council expressed this in different words, speaking of
infallibility, but it is the same message:

The body of the faithful as a whole, anointed as they are by the Holy One
(1 John 2:20, 27), cannot err in matters of belief. Thanks to a supernatural
sense of the faith which characterizes the People as a whole, it manifests

50   A PEOPLE OF PRIESTS

This fundamental conviction that the People of Israel had reached its full growth and had been renewed for all time by Christ is reflected in the exhortations given to the members of the restored People of God, as the New Testament writers draw out its implications:

> In other words, brothers, through the blood of Jesus we have the right to enter the sanctuary, by a new way which he has opened for us, a living opening through the curtain, that is to say, his body. And we have the supreme high priest over all the house of God. So as we go in, let us be sincere in heart and filled with faith, our minds sprinkled and free from any trace of bad conscience and our bodies washed with pure water. Let us keep firm in the hope we profess, because the one who made the promise is faithful. Let us be concerned for each other, to stir a response in love and good works. Do not stay away from the meetings of the community, as some do, but encourage each other to go; the more so as you see the Day drawing near. (Heb. 10:19–25)

The Epistle to the Hebrews is not talking of something that exists only in the mind, an ideal to be meditated upon in private devotion, but of a real community of living people. There is a clear reference to the baptism by which they entered that community; since they now have the 'right to enter the sanctuary', hitherto reserved to the official priests, it is evident that by that baptism they have all now become

---

this unerring quality when 'from the bishops down to the last member of the laity' (St Augustine, *De Praed. Sanct.*, 14, 27, PL 44, 980) it shows universal agreement in matters of faith and morals (*L.G.*, n. 12).

All are able to bear common witness, because all are 'taught by God'. Infallibility belongs to the Church as a whole, because all are held together in one body by the same faith. Together, the whole Church presents an unfailing witness as well as offering acceptable worship.

PRIESTS IN CHRIST

51

priests of God. The work of Christ opens the way to the direct access of all to the Eucharist, the worship of the New Israel. Believers are truly 'within the sanctuary', able to rest assured that their daily life in harmony with the New Law is accepted by God as true worship. This means a concern for one another in love and good works (10:24) and at the same time attendance at the regular meetings of the community (10:25).

The sacrifice of Christ, our new life in him, and the worship we offer make up one reality. Their union and interdependence is repeatedly affirmed in the Epistle to the Hebrews: '... the blood of Christ, who offered himself as the perfect sacrifice to God through the eternal Spirit, can purify our inner self from dead actions, so that we do our service to the living God' (Heb. 9:14). Personal renewal has a practical effect, spoken of in priestly terms as authentic worship.

There is no indication whatsoever in the Epistle to the Hebrews that those who offer worship and are the priests of the New Covenant are divided and distinguished from one another as far as their priesthood is concerned. Christ is the mediator of a priesthood which is given indifferently to all. The disciples of Christ are addressed by God as sons (Heb. 12:5–8), and love one another like brothers (Heb. 13:1).

But the community does have leaders, who are responsible for 'preaching the Word of God' and who are to be obeyed: 'Remember your leaders, those who spoke to you the word of God ... Obey your leaders and submit to them; for they are keeping watch over your souls, as men who will have to give account' (Heb. 13:7, 17). Within the one people, there are some with special responsibility for teaching and government. They are not spoken of as priests; it is notable that the image that occurs to the author when speaking of them is the image of shepherd:

I pray that the God of peace, who brought our Lord Jesus

back from the dead to become the great Shepherd of the sheep by the blood that sealed an eternal covenant, may make you ready to do his will in any kind of good action; and turn us all into whatever is acceptable to himself through Jesus Christ, to whom be glory for ever and ever, Amen. (Heb. 13:20–1)

The reference to the Shepherd, the Pastor, who has care of his sheep and makes possible our obedience to the will of God, with its special significance for those who in his service are given a share in his concern for them, is the key to the proper understanding of the ordained ministry within the community of worshippers.

A Real Offering, Made by Real Priests

In speaking of the worship that is offered by the Christian believer as a priest of God, the Epistle to the Hebrews knows nothing of any split between 'inner' and 'outer', between public and private. 'Do not stay away from the meetings of the community, as some do' (10:25). Going to the meetings is part of the believers' 'concern for one another'. The worship God finds acceptable (12:28) keeps 'words' and 'works' together. Liturgical worship, as we would say, and correspondence with God's will in our daily lives are inseparable from one another. We both offer to God 'an unending sacrifice of praise, a verbal sacrifice that is offered every time we acknowledge his name' (13:15), and 'keep doing good works and sharing [our] resources' (13:16).

Further to this, any tendency that we might have to think of the sacrifice offered by every Christian as a sacrifice in some diluted or subordinate sense fails to match up to the affirmations of Hebrews, as it does to the words of St Paul to the Romans: 'Think of God's mercy, my brothers, and

PRIESTS IN CHRIST 53

worship him, I beg you, in a way that is worthy of thinking beings, by offering your living bodies as a holy sacrifice, truly pleasing to God' (12:1). This passage from St Paul was used in the conciliar Constitution on the Church, *Lumen Gentium*, which gathers together (n. 10) some of the most important New Testament texts on the priesthood conferred upon all members of the People of God. Christ our High Priest has enabled us to offer spiritual sacrifices and to proclaim the power of him who has called us from darkness to light. As we have seen (Introduction p. 9), this affirmation of the general priesthood of all the faithful precedes the Council's treatment of the 'ministerial or hierarchical priesthood' in this document. It must always be borne in mind as a qualification without distinction in virtue of which each member of the Church, ordained or not, has the same ability to worship God conferred upon them. Baptism makes everyone who receives it a part of the 'spiritual house and holy priesthood' that offers this worship.

One Priesthood, Not Two

This strong affirmation of the common priesthood of all the faithful, the first in any conciliar document, contrasts with a number of different attempts on the part of theologians to explain the relationship between the ministers whom for centuries they have been accustomed to call priests and the other members of the Church.

Are all those who have been ordained, priests in the 'proper' sense, for instance, while the rest of the faithful are priests in a 'figurative' sense? Nothing in the text allows us to draw that conclusion. The baptized are priests in the full sense of the word, since in Christ they can offer the kind of worship that the Old Testament system of worship prefigured

54 A PEOPLE OF PRIESTS

and that God desired: an offering of themselves together with the offering of Christ through his gift of the Eucharist.

Or can the use of the term 'spiritual' of the common priesthood's worship be taken to mean that their offering is in some sense inferior to a 'real' offering made by the ordained minister? A distinction of this kind would downgrade the status of the Spirit, who is the agent conferring reality on the offerings made by the faithful. This is not a sacrifice in some diminished sense. 'Spiritual', in the Christian context, means 'real'. In this context, it is not appropriate to make the distinction.

The Catechism of the Council of Trent speaks of an 'exterior' and an 'interior' offering, but these terms cannot be used to provide distinct labels, as if there were two offerings. The ministers' offering is exterior and public, certainly, but it also has its interior force and effect, while the rest of the faithful, by their presence at the Eucharist and by their witness, join in offering the same 'exterior' act of worship and praise. 'Public' and 'private' fall under the same criticism.

Can one say that one priesthood is sacramental, while the other is non-sacramental? Since the common priesthood is exercised in virtue of the sacrament of baptism which all have received, it is certainly sacramental; once again, the distinction will not hold.

Talk of priesthood 'in the full sense of the word' and of an 'incomplete' or 'shared' priesthood is equally unsatisfactory. It is Christ who is our unique High Priest 'in the full sense of the word', and all other priesthood, baptized as well as ordained, is a share in his priesthood.

It has even been suggested that the masculine-feminine distinction could be used: the clergy with their masculine priesthood and the laity with their feminine priesthood. Comment would be superfluous on such a curiosity, which appears to be a wry comment on parochial worship as it is sometimes to be found. Theologically, it would seem to exclude

PRIESTS IN CHRIST

the clergy from membership of the Church as the Bride of Christ.[2]

The failure of these attempts to grapple with the distinction surely points to the conclusion that the fundamental affirmation, the overriding thought, must be of the unity of the priesthood received from Christ. Throughout, it is the same priesthood, in which all must feel the same solidarity. Each person exercises that priesthood in a different way; everyone is essentially different from everyone else, both in their human make-up and in the special gifts they have been given for the service of the Kingdom of God. Those who receive the sacrament of ordination find their priesthood given a special character, which distinguishes it from the priesthood of others by the responsibility it holds within God's plan of salvation, not by any superimposed philosophical or sociological categories. The unity of the whole priesthood of Christ must remain the dominant theme.

Nothing must be allowed to weaken the force of the message of these New Testament writers, with all its implications. The priesthood desired by God and foreshadowed in the Old Testament has now been made available to all: in Christ, we have been given the grace to serve God in our daily lives. Together and individually, we are now able to live in harmony with the gospel and so give glory to the God who made us and saved us. Anything that is said of the ordained ministry must not undermine the fundamental reality of the one priesthood of Christ; it is the context within which the ministry must work, the pattern of relationships that the ministry must establish. Whatever the differences arising out of ethnic origin, culture, politics or any other source, in the Church we are made one, a single 'line of kings

---

[2]This discussion is indebted to Mgr Philips' commentary on *Lumen Gentium*, *L'Eglise et son Mystère au Deuxième Concile du Vatican*, 1967, I, 146.

56 A PEOPLE OF PRIESTS

and priests'; 'everyone is a "first-born son" and a citizen of heaven' (Heb. 12:23).

Anything less than this, any introduction of classifications that obscure the unity of this one chorus of worship, the offering of the true praise of a holy life, will not just damage the internal and external organization of this holy people; it will diminish the force of the gospel itself, weakening our understanding of the extent of Christ's victory and the overwhelming nature of his gift. The New Testament writers declare that the promise made to Moses, 'I will count you a kingdom of priests, a consecrated nation' (Exod. 19:6), has now definitively come true. To superimpose divisions once again, to give class distinctions a place in the citizenship of heaven, or to weaken our conviction that by grace we have free access, each one personally, to the acceptable worship of God, would be to nullify the work of Christ, making it appear that we still live under the Old Testament and that he has not yet come to complete his saving work.

The People of God

> ... You are a chosen race, a royal priesthood, a consecrated nation, a people set apart [RSV: God's own people] to sing the praises of God who called you out of darkness into his wonderful light. Once you were not a people at all and now you are the People of God. (*laos Theou*; 1 Pet. 2:9–10)

This image was chosen by the Second Vatican Council as the theme of Chapter II of its Dogmatic Constitution on the Church, so as to situate the Church among the innumerable peoples of the world and at the same time indicate its potentiality as the gathering point of human unity, restored and to be completed in Christ. As with 'priesthood', so with 'people': the call to membership of the People of God estab-

PRIESTS IN CHRIST 57

lishes all who receive it as full members of the community which they join. Distinctions arising out of natural characteristics or out of special divine gifts or responsibilities must never obscure our awareness of the fundamental unity that we have received. The People of God are not only one in their uniqueness as a human society; they are internally united, one in the equal partnership they offer to all who belong to them.

It must therefore always be borne in mind that the word *laos*, people, designates the whole People of God without distinction, not a particular part of that People, however important, and that this fact is central to Christian faith. The passage from 1 Peter quoted above goes on to link the existence of God's People with redemption itself: 'once you were outside the mercy and now you have been given mercy' (1 Pet. 2:10). So the force of the term 'People of God' is not simply that of an invitation to join a particular organization. Far more radically than that, it is God's forgiveness of our sin that enables us to belong to his People. Solidarity in sin – which means the confusion, division and hostility that afflict the human race generation after generation – has been replaced through God's mercy by the solidarity of his People, living in a shared understanding, harmony and love. Forgiveness for all is a gift freely offered to all, not a special privilege reserved for a few. Our awareness of common citizenship (Heb. 12:23) stems from our knowledge that all have sinned and all have been forgiven. One priesthood, one people; these are realities that derive from our salvation by Christ. They are the real result of God's action in response to our need, and they continue to convey that response to others, bringing them with us into the same priesthood and the same people.

Since this membership of the People of God through the restoration of the unity of the human race, shattered by sin, is the direct consequence of the salvation of which all stand in need, it should underlie all our thinking about the Church, its aims and its modes of action. The reform of the Church's life requires a correction of those categories and modes of thought that can obscure the true character of the reality in which we are involved. Many of our difficulties arise from an unexamined use of distinctions and divisions which we have inherited without questioning their authenticity.

The current use of the word 'laity', derived from *laos*, in conjunction and in contrast with 'clergy', derived from *kleros*, is an obvious example of the substitution of a limited, culture-related vision of human and Church affairs for the God-given reality.

We have seen that *laos*, 'people', was used originally of the whole People of God without distinction; but the word derived from it, 'laity' has shrunk, so to speak, to designate a group, albeit the largest group, in God's People.

The same shift has taken place over the centuries in the use of the word *kleros*. In 1 Peter, the term is used of all the members of the Church who are assigned to the pastoral care of the elders:

> Now I have something to tell your elders: I am an elder myself and a witness to the sufferings of Christ, and with you I have a share in the glory that is to be revealed. Be the shepherds of the flock that is entrusted to you: watch over it ... Never be a dictator over any group that is put in your charge [*kleros*], but be an example that the whole flock can follow. (1 Pet. 5:1–3)

The word is used to denote a chosen portion, set apart as the inherited possession or responsibility of a particular person or group. In other words, in modern terms, it designates the laity! The process of history has turned the word upside-down, so that now the 'chosen portion' are the shepherds, not the sheep, the carers, not those committed to their care. Instead of applying to the whole Church, as the chosen ones of God, or, under God, to the portion of his flock assigned to particular pastors, it has come to refer to the pastors

PRIESTS IN CHRIST 59

themselves, serving to set them apart and marking them off from those for whom they are meant to care.

It is true that the word was also used to designate particular groups as specially chosen by God: the *kleros* of the martyrs, for example. In its current restriction, and its use over the centuries in contradistinction from the laity, one must however see a damaging reversal of the meaning originally conveyed.

Since the Second Vatican Council, the Church has already moved towards reducing the factors which contribute to the clergy's sense of being a group sharply marked off from the rest of the Church. The ceremony of the first tonsure, whereby a candidate's hair was clipped as a sign of his dedication and his transfer from the lay to the clerical state, has been abolished. The minor orders of porter, reader, acolyte and exorcist, which were given only to those preparing for ordination, creating a step-by-step approach to the diaconate and presbyterate and thereby encouraging the understanding of hierarchy in terms of ascending rank, have also been abolished. So there has been certain shrinking of the clerical state, which is now entered at the diaconate. Further reflection may well conclude that the notion is inappropriate at any stage, and that the pastoral relationship requires a strong sense of close identity with the whole priestly people of God.

It has been suggested[3] that Chapter 2 of *Lumen Gentium*, on the People of God, abolished the word 'laity'. Instead, it makes us think of a single body consisting of all the baptized, who 'by regeneration and the anointing of the Holy Spirit, are consecrated into a spiritual house and a holy priesthood' (*L.G.* n. 10). And in his magisterial commentary on *Lumen Gentium*, Mgr G. Philips of the University of Louvain, dealing with Chapter 4, remarks that it is to be hoped that in future it will not be necessary to have separate chapters on the laity and the clergy.

60 A PEOPLE OF PRIESTS

If one starts from the separation of clergy and laity into two classes as a fact of life with which one has to work, and then seeks their closer collaboration, demarcation disputes inevitably arise, as they have done in the past, for example, over the apostolate of the laity, and as they are doing at the present moment over priesthood itself. We need to start from what we are and what we have in common, and remain aware of it throughout our analysis of the respective roles in the Church; otherwise, we shall overlook the very basis of our collaboration, and find ourselves using artificial and external means of organizing our joint action.

A recent Roman document on the vocation and mission of the laity, *Christifideles Laici*, an Apostolic Exhortation of Pope John Paul II, published in 1988 and based upon the work of the Roman Synod of 1986, may be taken as representative of the Church's thinking on this subject in recent years. It suffers from the fundamental ambiguity that arises when the same term is used for the reality that involves us all and for a specific part of that reality.

Its opening sentence, referring to 'The lay members of Christ's faithful people', and speaking of these lay members as 'part of the People of God', betrays this ambiguity from the start.

If 'lay' is used in this partial way, marking off those who are not pastors, priests, deacons and religious from those who are (n. 7), it inevitably loses its full force. Precisely because of the centuries-old clergy/laity distinction, it inevitably takes on the current meaning of 'non-professional', 'amateur', 'unlearned', 'unskilled', even 'unsanctified' and 'secular'; worse still, it has widely carried since the nineteenth

---

[3]By Henry Holstein SJ, in his preface to P. Guilmot SJ, *Fin d'une Eglise Cléricale?*, Paris, Cerf, 1969, p. 10: 'In my opinion, this chapter amounts to the abolition of the equivocal and rather disagreeable word "laity" '.

PRIESTS IN CHRIST 61

century the meaning of 'anti-clerical', 'neutral or hostile where religion is concerned, especially the Catholic religion'.

However much one tries to rescue the word from its present significance, to promote the group concerned and to encourage their full participation in the work of the gospel, one will still be left with the feeling that we have here a lower-rank group. And if they start there, they will remain there, whatever the exhortations of the clergy.

As is to be expected, other documents of the Church reveal the unresolved questions and differences of emphasis and opinion that are still with us. One section of *Lumen Gentium* (Chapter 4, n. 32) lays particularly strong emphasis on the unity of the People of God and on the place of the ordained ministers within that People:

> If therefore everyone in the Church does not proceed by the same path, nevertheless all are called to sanctity and have received an equal privilege of faith through the justice of God (2 Pet. 1:1). And if by the will of Christ some are made teachers, dispensers of mysteries, shepherds on behalf of others, yet all share a true equality with regard to the dignity and to the activity common to all the faithful for the building up of the Body of Christ.

A similar difference of texture is to be found in Chapter 2 of *Christifideles Laici*, which deals with the ministries and charisms exercised within the communion of the Church, and only uses the word 'clergy' once, in the statement that the lay faithful, together with the clergy and women and men religious make up the one People of God; the word 'lay' does in fact often occur in this chapter, but it could have been left out entirely without invalidating the chapter's teaching.

The clergy/laity distinction is a cultural, not a theological one; it is foreign to the New Testament and has masked the inner unity of the Church. Properly speaking, to be 'of

62 A PEOPLE OF PRIESTS

the church' is to be 'lay': someone dedicated to the gathering together of the People of God.

To promote the work of the Church in the world as the joint task of all members, one must remember that in the People of God there is a single class, and that in that context all are priests of God, each worshipping him according to the manner in which they respond to their individual vocation in the world.[4]

More reflection on the common priesthood and the worship we share is needed if we are to resolve the problems that arise in the allocation of duties in the mission of the Church; it would help us to see more clearly our respective roles and our joint collaboration.

Sacred and Secular

Just as we still suffer from an insufficiently examined perpetuation of the clergy/laity distinction as we have inherited it from the past, so also there is a hesitation over the use of the sacred/secular categories. While *Christifideles Laici* (n. 15) declares, following Vatican II (*Lumen Gentium* n. 32), that all members of the People of God 'share a common dignity from their birth in Christ, . . . the same filial grace and the same vocation to perfection', it is also said that the lay faithful have a manner of life, described as the 'secular character', which is properly and particularly theirs. Here the document echoes *Lumen Gentium* n. 31; n. 32 lays greater stress on the unity and 'common dignity' of all.

---

[4]The Pope refers in *Christifideles Laici* to words he used at the beginning of his pastoral ministry: 'He who was born of the Virgin Mary, the carpenter's son – as he was thought to be – Son of the living God (confessed by Peter), has come to make us "a kingdom of priests".' He intended, he said, to 'emphasise forcefully the priestly, prophetic and kingly dignity of the entire People of God'. It would have been a better document if that thought had been pursued more consistently.

PRIESTS IN CHRIST

This paragraph of *Christifideles Laici* (n. 15) makes an affirmation which betrays a certain obscurity in need of further unravelling. It states that this manner of life of the lay faithful 'sets a person apart, without, however, bringing about a separation from the ministerial priesthood or from men and women religious'. This 'setting apart without separation' points to a tension that, as we have just seen, was already present in the chapter on the laity in *Lumen Gentium*. The author seems to be taking back what he has just affirmed; there is room here for further reflection. Is 'setting apart' the right expression? Within the body, the members are indeed specialized, but they are also closely interdependent.

If the categories of sacred and secular, church and world, are too sharply distinguished from one another, then separations are inevitable, and however hard one tries to relate the groups under discussion in healthy collaboration, they can never be fully integrated in one harmonious common action.

But the gospel does integrate the two groups in question, from the start. The parable of the workers in the vineyard, restricted selectively by *Christifideles Laici* to the laity ('that part of the People of God which might be likened to the labourers in the vineyard mentioned in St Matthew's Gospel' (n. 1)), applies in the first place, as the document also declares, without reflecting further on the fact, to 'every person who comes into this world' (n. 2).

This hesitation between a view of the whole Church as sharing a common vocation and the restriction of a term that applies to us all to a particular part of the Church, will need to be eliminated if collaboration based on our unity in Christ is to be achieved.

The exhortation quotes some words of Pope Paul VI, declaring that the Church 'has an authentic secular dimension, inherent to her inner nature and mission, which is deeply rooted in the mystery of the Word Incarnate, and which is realized in different forms through her members' (n. 15). Paul

VI clearly maintains that it is the whole Church that has this 'authentic secular dimension'; but the document, following Vatican II in this, seems reluctant to develop the full bearing of his teaching, and assigns the term 'secular' 'properly and particularly to the lay faithful'.

> The world thus becomes the place and the means for the lay faithful to fulfil their Christian vocation. (*C.L.*, no. 15)

> What can be an additional or exceptional task for those who belong to the ordained ministry is the typical mission of the lay faithful. (John Paul II, Angelus talk, 15 March 1987, quoted in *C.L.*, note 40)

The grounds on which this restriction is made call for re-examination, since they lead to an unwarranted narrowing-down of many of the statements of the New Testament. In *Christifideles Laici* n. 15, for example, we find it said that: 'The images of salt, light and heaven, taken from the Gospel, although indiscriminately applicable to all Jesus's disciples, are specifically applied to the lay faithful.' Why 'indiscriminately'? Why this somewhat disparaging term? What are the grounds of this limitation? It would be better to give the gospel its full force. The exhortation treats these scriptural images in the same way as it did the parable of the workers in the vineyard.

In his *Jalons pour une Théologie du Laïcat*, Yves Congar wrote that a proper treatment of the laity requires 'a total ecclesiology'.[5] The full implications of the remark have still to be worked out. One will have to start from the unity of the Church and the cooperation of all its members; as soon as the laity are written about as if they were a race apart, distortion sets in. One must never lose sight of the unity of

---

[5]'Au fond, il n'y aurait qu'une théologie valable: une ecclésiologie totale.' 'Fundamentally, the only valid theology [sc.: of the laity] would be a total ecclesiology.' *ibid.*, Paris, 1954, 13.

PRIESTS IN CHRIST 65

the Church as a People and the unity of its mission, which is to glorify God through the true orientation and transformation of everything that he has made. 'The Church, at once "a visible assembly and a spiritual community", marches with the whole of humanity, shares the fortunes of the world here below, exists as the leaven, we might say the soul, of human society, to renew it in Christ and transform it into God's family' (*Gaudium et Spes*, n. 40). The 'leaven' is the power of the Risen Christ, both temporal, or material, and spiritual, not 'above' the world, but an order of existence, a total life, that works within the world to transform it as a whole. There is no service of the Risen Christ which is not service of the world he has raised up.

All members of the Church, all servants of Christ, live in the world, and cannot live as if they were out of it. All our actions have a secular effect. Those who are ordained to a particular ministry or those who are called to the religious life have an undoubted effect in this world, and they would be wasting their time if they did not. To be an enclosed nun is to make a personal statement about life in this world that does most certainly change things for everyone else that sees and understands: a statement about priorities. A society with such people in its midst is profoundly different from a society that knows nothing of worship and prayer.

The ministry of the Church is not carried out in some sort of vacuum, in a state existing alongside 'the world' where the non-ordained work. To teach Christianity, to gather together and organize a Christian people, to lead them to devote their lives to the worship of Almighty God, all of this changes the world. It has a political and social effect. The ministry of the Church cannot be undertaken without material means, without property and without money; administration in that field also has its influence in the public domain.

Rather than making tasks 'additional' or 'exceptional' for some and 'typical' for others, it would be truer to the nature

A PEOPLE OF PRIESTS

of the Church to see all her members as having a single overriding purpose – to give glory to God – and within that unity to recognize an immense diversity of gifts and forms of service, each of which in one way or another benefits society as a whole.

Someone who is chosen as a bishop, presbyter or deacon to build up the Christian people, to lead and serve a community made one in Christ, cannot take sides, favouring one class or party more than another, unless it be the side of those who have no party, the side of the poor and the weak. Those who have not been given that particular responsibility will be right to take sides and to defend special interests in order to achieve legitimate goals for the benefit of society, provided they always acknowledge that they are working as members of the community as a whole and in the service of that community. To make sure that there is such a community embracing everyone and in which everyone can find their home is the work of the ordained ministry. Both sorts of ministry are 'secular', since both contribute to the just ordering of the affairs of the world.

The ordained ministers of the Church must know that by sticking strictly to their brief – building up the Church by teaching the gospel, obeying it themselves, inspiring and guiding others to follow it, celebrating the sacraments that relate us to God and to one another in Christ – they are having an effect in the world, a secular effect. They are resisting all those who work for themselves rather than for God. They stand in the way of such people, by promoting an understanding of human life that denies their right to do as they will with a world they regard as their private possession.

It is a mistake therefore to attempt to work with a classification of members of the Church into those who have a 'secular' vocation and those who do not. All are in this world and are part of it; the differences are to be found in the particular means of action and the special tasks that are

PRIESTS IN CHRIST 67

assigned to each individual person. Unless the fundamental unity of all is constantly remembered, a division is introduced which hinders cooperation and, worse still, adds to the factors leading to conflict among human beings, as the clergy/laity distinction and separation undoubtedly has for many centuries.

The appropriateness of the term 'secular' to describe the diocesan clergy or those who are not members of a religious order is being widely questioned in the light of fresh thinking on this theme, and is discussed in Chapter 4.

The House of God

> It is true that Moses was faithful in the house of God, as a servant, acting as witness to the things which were to be divulged later; but Christ was faithful as a son, and as the master in the house. And we are his house, as long as we cling to our hope with the confidence that we glory in. (Heb. 3:5–6)

The New Testament image of the house and of the family and household who live there needs more attention than is usually given to it as a guide to our understanding of the community of Christ. The stewardship parables take on particular force when they are related to the family of the Church, and seen not simply as moral exhortations to good management in general, but as a commentary on actual human relationships in an identifiable society.

A reading of 1 Peter will show how this image was understood as applying to really existing communities, with all their variety and reciprocal relationships and duties. Through personal discipleship and faith in Christ – 'set yourselves close to him' – individuals are brought together in a holy priesthood offering spiritual sacrifices and 'making a spiritual house' (*oikos pneumatikos*: 1 Pet. 2:4, 5). The house image relates to the Old Testament tradition ('Moses was faithful in the house of God') and the gospel use of the theme; it also relates to the families and households that were taking on a Christian character and becoming the local churches of Asia Minor.

The Church was growing through the acceptance of the gospel in particular families, which would include not only the parents and children, but the servants, slave and free, the associates in family trades or businesses, and others who depended on them for friendship and support. The relationships in the Church at large were to be modelled on this all-embracing family life, which itself was to be raised to a new level through the influence of gospel principles.

The 'spiritual house' of which 1 Peter speaks (2:5) was a real community, a household, a family, for which definite rules of conduct and principles of moral and social life were prescribed. Christianity was spreading through its acceptance by families and through meetings in private houses. Houses provided the sociological base as well as the theological image for the Church. 'Aquila and Prisca, with the church that meets at their house, send you their warmest wishes in the Lord', wrote St Paul (1 Cor. 16:19; cf. Rom. 16:5, Philem. 2, Col. 4:15). In the Acts of the Apostles, there are four cases of the conversion of families following upon that of the head of the family (Cornelius, 10; Lydia, 16:15; the gaoler at Philippi, 16:29–34; Crispus at Corinth, 18:8). This would include servants and others associated with the house as well as children and other relatives.

The 'people of priests', while it was drawn from every nation and social class, was not on that account an 'invisible' group, only detectable when it met together, a group without permanent corporate existence. It was rooted in real families, who gave it a local, recognizable existence and provided the structure and the model for its life as a community. It was

PRIESTS IN CHRIST

the good fathers of families who had proved themselves to be appropriate candidates for pastoral oversight (1 Timothy, Titus).

The exhortations concerning family relationships, both public and private, in 1 Peter 2 and 3 show that the Church was not a private society of like-minded individuals, confined to particular age-groups or classes, pursuing a limited aim; it demonstrated its family character by embracing all the members of particular families in the fullest sense of that word, and gave them a common purpose. It was firm and solid (a house built on a rock; cf. Matt. 7:24–7), providing a real foundation for those who believed and proving a stumbling block to those who refused belief (1 Pet. 2:8).

Finally, the household supplied more than the substantial sociological expression of the Church's life and moral principles. The house envisaged in 1 Peter was the house of God (1 Pet. 4:17), and so his Temple, in which a holy priesthood offered spiritual sacrifices (1 Pet. 2:4, 5). Coming to live among his People in the House that he was building through the power of the Spirit, Christ being the cornerstone, God had enabled them to offer true sacrifices. 'Living honourably among the pagans' (1 Pet. 2:12) was the true worship now offered in the Temple that was the Body of Christ.

A Diversity of Gifts

One People of God, one Family of God, in which all have an equal right to be present, and all can feel equally at home: this is not achieved through imposing a set pattern, through mechanical drill and forced uniformity. Essential to the feeling at home is the knowledge that one is accepted with all the individuality that marks one off from others. Each different part of the Body has its contribution to make. This applies to all the differences, whether physical, racial, or cultural, that distinguish us. It also applies to the many special gifts by way of intellectual and spiritual competence that are needed to build up the church.

It is in this context that the attempt to characterize the gift of ordained ministry must be placed. In his list of these gifts (1 Cor. 12:27–30), St Paul mentions the apostles as having the first place, and it is from the group of the Apostles, who were called to a special relationship with Christ and a share in his mission, that this ministry, with its concern for the whole gospel message and for the whole Church, will develop.

The Sacrifice of Praise

The common orientation of all Christians, beyond mission and beyond service, is worship. If this aim – the glory given to God by lives transformed and therefore able to worship him in praise and self-offering – is forgotten, the Church's life turns in on itself and problems of chain of command, of organizing and directing, become more acute. There must be a shared purpose beyond ourselves. We do not preach mission simply in order to fill our churches. We do not see even the care given to human need as an end in itself. Without worship, the Church becomes one more pressure group and service promotes self-righteousness.

If we are putting the will of God first, are drawn by his love, and remember the perfection by which we are judged, then in mission and service we shall seek the other's growth in grace, the other's healing, not our own. That is why the Church is described in the New Testament as a people of priests, but not as a people of apostles, or even of servants.

Lumen Gentium gathered together the whole life of Christ's disciples under the heading of worship:

Through all these works befitting Christian men they can

PRIESTS IN CHRIST

offer spiritual sacrifices and proclaim the power of him who has called them out of darkness into his marvellous light (1 Pet. 2:4–10). Therefore all the disciples of Christ, persevering in prayer and praising God (Acts 2:42–7) should present themselves as a living sacrifice, holy and pleasing to God (Rom 12:1). (*L.G.* 10)

The next paragraph affirms that this self-offering takes place in the eucharistic sacrifice, in which all play their proper part – 'not, indeed, in the same way but each in that way which is appropriate to himself'. It is clear that all – bishops, presbyters and deacons with everyone else – offer the one sacrifice together.

And this offering that all make together is not a ceremonial substitute for inadequate offerings made in the efforts and achievements of our daily life. It is the reality that makes everything else real, consecrating our personal offerings and therefore making them acceptable in themselves. Once our life in the week is linked with that Sunday eucharist, then it takes on its proper orientation. The eucharistic assembly, by bringing together the whole people of God, puts us in our place within the full reality of the human race as God has made us. We open our hearts and minds to the reality of Christ, who corrects our faults and enlarges our limitations; by sharing in his authentic life we shed our flaws and our falsehood and are restored to the everlasting friendship of God.

3

Christ and the Apostles

God sent his Son into the world not to condemn the world
but so that through him the world might be saved. (John
3:17)

The presence of a special ministry of bishops, presbyters and
deacons within the priesthood of the whole Church and as a
permanent feature of her life must find its origin and justification within the life and work of Christ himself.

Christ always spoke and acted as one who had been sent
among us; he was a messenger, a representative, an ambassador. And he in his turn sent out others. It is there, if anywhere,
that the source of this special ministry must be found. This
chapter will examine the relationship between Christ and his
Apostles as the necessary indicator of the continuing character of his mission.

The credentials of an ambassador depend upon the person
he or she represents; Christ's standing derived from the Father
who sent him and from his faithfulness to that representation.

This theme, that his life was devoted to doing the will of
the one who had sent him, runs through the whole story
of his life and continues in the life of the Church, fruit of his
obedience. An apostle is someone sent with a message; Christ
was an apostle; he chose and named his apostles, whom he
sent into the world as he had been sent; the Church they

CHRIST AND THE APOSTLES 73

continue to build is apostolic, sent into every corner of the
world, in every generation.

> 'I came not of my own accord, but he sent me.' (John 8:42
> RSV)

> The spirit of the Lord has been given to me; for he has
> anointed me. He has sent me to bring the good news to the
> poor. (Luke 4:18)

> 'This is working for God: you must believe in the one he
> has sent.' (John 6:29)

He had to show that he represented God, and to do that he
had himself to be faithful to God's commands, and so to the
task that he had been given. Christ called upon his hearers to
believe in that sending: to recognize that he was not delivering
a message that he had made up by himself, but one from the
Creator, his heavenly Father. So closely did his life correspond
with what he had been sent to say and do that he himself
could be said to be the message, the living Word of God.

Others had been sent, angels, prophets, John the Baptist;
here finally was the Son, the one of whom all other messengers had spoken; he was the burden of their messages, the
confirmation of the truth of God's words to us and, through
his achievement, the final accomplishment of God's purpose
for us.

Immediately after announcing his mission, Christ began to
collect around himself a group that he would call his Apostles,
the ones who were sent (Luke 6:14). It was an appropriate
title for an office that was familiar enough, in the ancient
world as today. As he had been sent, so he sent them; the
name identified them with his own overriding purpose, with
his own 'being sent'. First Simon and Andrew, James and
John were called (Matt. 4:18–22); when the whole group of
the Twelve had been constituted, he sent them out, telling
them to do as he had done from the beginning of his public

A PEOPLE OF PRIESTS

mission: to proclaim that 'the kingdom of God is close at hand' (Matt. 4:17; 10:6).

This sending-out was an extension of his own sending-out: 'Anyone who welcomes you welcomes me; and those who welcome me welcome the one who sent me' (Matt. 10:40). Our Lord's conduct of his mission was not a solitary, individual affair. His choice of the Twelve and their association with him was an essential part of it. It belonged to the content and character of his message that it should be conveyed to the world through others who were his accredited representatives. It brought people into a speaking relationship with God and into a speaking relationship with one another.

His message was to be written on their hearts; they were his disciples, as were others, but they in particular received the full extent of what he had to say, since they were to be responsible for safeguarding and transmitting it. By accompanying him from the beginning to the end of his mission, they were made aware of everything that he had said and taught and were witnesses of his passion, death and resurrection.

His teaching of the Apostles was exemplary of all his teaching: going at their pace, letting the words sink in, and also berating them for their slowness and reluctance to understand, their 'hardness of heart'; but nevertheless keeping his confidence in them and entrusting himself and his message totally to them.

His use of the twelve Apostles as the special hearers of his teaching, bearers of his message and joint organizers, when need be, of the crowds that came to listen to him, was an indispensable expression of his own role as the Apostle of God. The message was to be heard publicly and in community; it gathered people together, helping them to live in due order and in harmony with one another. The Apostles were indicators of his messianic calling; they stood for the twelve tribes of Israel, and so for the whole people of God;

CHRIST AND THE APOSTLES 75

they would become the foundation stones of the New Israel (Rev. 21:14).

By choosing his Apostles and giving them their special role, Christ indicated his own place in history: the history that led up to his coming and the further history that would be made by his sending of the Apostles into the world. And their common life already showed what kind of a people the New Israel would be.

For the existence of the company of the Apostles made it clear that the New Covenant was one that was communicated and established by word of mouth, drawing people into conversation with one another. Christ's own teachings were given in that way, by formal delivery as well as by questioning and discussion among the Apostles and among all those who heard him and met him. He proclaimed his message for those 'who had ears to hear', in a memorable form; he was ready to respond when problems were put to him, and to give an impromptu lesson when the opportunity arose.

Their sharing was not confined to ideas; they helped others through their common purse, and when betrayal came, its depth was all the more grievous in that it was perpetrated by the one responsible for this practical expression of their solidarity with others.

So the twelve Apostles together revealed the character of the Church of the New Covenant. The make-up of the group – a former collaborator with the occupying power finding himself associating with a one-time terrorist – indicated in real life the way Christ intended to gather all parties, all mentalities, to himself. The group itself was thoroughly human, with its quarrels, its jealousies and rivalries, its devotion to its leader – and even its traitor. Jesus needed them to show who he was and what his purpose was, both during his teaching mission and after the resurrection, when he continued to instruct them and finally sent them out to represent him. Only at the culmination of the work he had been sent to do, from the agony in the Garden to the day of resurrection, were they dispersed, leaving him to act alone for the salvation of all. And even then, during those last days, their all-too-human attitudes made them truly representative figures: God's representatives, but also ours.

In all this, they constituted the beginning of the New Israel, the Church of the New Covenant, through their being personally called by Christ (the Church, the *ecclesia*, is the 'called' community) and through their being bound together not by a written law, but by a living person who spoke with them and gave his Spirit to them. They were a new People, with a new common language: the Word of God.

The cellular pattern of this community, gathered round its 'nucleus' in the person of Christ, is retained in the community that has continued its witness to Christ from the day of Pentecost onwards. Christ and the Apostles, then Peter and the Apostles: the simple fundamental pattern, characteristic of the cosmos at all levels, inorganic as well as organic, in the firmament as under the microscope, remains with the Church, marking her life in small communities as well as in her overall structure. The fulfilment of Christ's promise to be with his disciples 'always' is revealed in the structure of the groups that he shapes by his presence, a structure visible locally as well as overall, on the global scale.

The synoptic Gospels give the circumstances and the words in which the 'sending' of the Apostles was expressed. St John gives, very simply, the underlying theology, ' "As the Father sent me so am I sending you" ' (John 20:21). The Father's purpose is still to be carried through. Christ's work had included the choosing, teaching and training of the Apostles, and now, just as he was sent in the first place, he sends them in their turn. The apostolic group, called together to be a sign of the coming of the Messiah, will continue to represent him and thus will complete his work.

CHRIST AND THE APOSTLES 77

Given to Some, to be Shared by All

In all this, a gospel principle applies: the gifts of God are given to be shared. It is a principle governing the whole sacramental life of the Church, and is therefore fundamental to the situation and activity of the ordained priesthood within the general priesthood of the Body of Christ. Failure to grasp and to apply this principle has in the past led to theories of the ordained ministry that either overstressed its rights and privileges or else did away with it altogether.

The Apostles were disciples, learning from Christ; but they were not the only disciples. They were part of a wider group. The Gospels remind us of this by calling them 'the disciples' as well as 'the Apostles' from time to time. They could not be Apostles if they were not first of all disciples, and remained disciples.

The Apostles were of course representatives who had been specially commissioned. But they were not the only representatives; and part of their mission was their duty to convey that fact to the world. Christ was represented by children (Luke 9:46–8), and others, not 'one of us', could act in his name (Luke 9:49–50). At the Last Judgement, the poor and the weak of every kind will be found to have been his representatives (Matt. 25:31–46). The Church herself, called together to receive the gift of salvation, and secure in her role as the mediator of guaranteed salvation, proclaims to the world, in the words of St Peter, that wherever people do what is right, they are acceptable to God (Acts 10:35).

God's gifts are given to some and not to others, and they are given to be shared: the gospel principle is everywhere at work. The fact that there were many disciples, and that Peter and Andrew, James and John and the others took their places among them, does not mean that they were not also chosen for special responsibility: to be the guardians of the message they had learnt and so to care for their fellow disciples. It is, after all, significant that those who were first called to follow Jesus, and thus to set the pattern of discipleship, were also chosen to become members of the group of Apostles; in them, both the general class and the special class of disciples are represented. And to carry the principle further, the fact that children, along with the weak, the poor and the needy of all kinds could represent Christ, just as well as the Apostles represented him, does not exclude the special choice of the Apostles for the duty of conveying that truth to the world; their gift was to be shared with many others.

The simple fact of Christ's choice of 'Simon whom he called Peter, and his brother Andrew; James, John, Philip, Bartholomew, Matthew, Thomas, James, son of Alphaeus, Simon called the Zealot, Judas son of James, and Judas who became a traitor' (Luke 6:14–16) is enough to establish that there is what Vatican II called an 'essential difference' (*L.G.* n. 10) between this group and the rest of the disciples. They were in a special position of responsibility from the moment of their first calling right through to the day of Pentecost and the growth of the Church that followed. They were the ones picked out to be with him and to bear witness eventually to the resurrection (Acts 1:22). They were chosen for this particular task, and others were not. That alone marked them off. But all of that was a gift to be shared: the knowledge he had given them, the powers of healing, the right to reconcile, the strength to build. Even their personal oversight of the Church was to be shared; others would be brought into their fellowship. Only one thing could not be shared; their uniqueness in being themselves, the ones whose lives were spent in walking with Christ before and after the Cross and in proclaiming what they had seen and heard to the world, so that others might have communion with them (1 John 1:3). And all that does not mean that they were better disciples than the others; by the grace of God and their own free response, they were, quite simply, different.

CHRIST AND THE APOSTLES

The difference, then, arises out of the Lord's choice, a choice also affirmed by St Paul at the opening of his epistles. It was a choice that conferred on them particular responsibilities, a character in accordance with those responsibilities and a distinctive relationship with him, with one another, with all those called to be his disciples, and with the world to which they were sent. And because it came from the Lord, it was permanent; God does not revoke his decisions nor withdraw his gifts.

The Work of the Apostles: the Defining Images

The title that indicates their purpose in and for the Church is, then, apostle; they were messengers, representatives, ambassadors. They were sent out by Christ, as he had been sent out, to proclaim the gospel (Matt. 28:19; John 20:21). And the way in which they were to do this was indicated by Christ and by themselves by the use of a number of images, familiar in Scripture and familiar in everyday life. They were images also used to convey the nature of the Church as a community related to God, and as such they were specially picked out in the conciliar decree *Lumen Gentium*. The Church is a sheepfold, a flock, a field, a vine to be cultivated, a building, the bride of Christ; and images drawn from these contexts are the ones used to indicate the work entrusted to the Apostles.

Fishermen and Shepherds

By calling the Apostles, right at the start, fishermen (Matt. 4:18–20), Christ chose an image of world-wide reference, in no way restricted to the particular world of the people of Israel. Fishermen have been known throughout human history; they ensure human survival, and they work in the seas, rivers and lakes of the world, not in temples made by human hands. The first Apostles were fishermen; they were not chosen from among the priests. They set the style for the others, who were not to model themselves on priests with their ritual functions, however necessary and respected their office, but on fishermen who went out to gather in their catch from the waters of the world. In that role, their nets would be cast for a human harvest.

Next, Christ used another image of the same kind, familiar in Greco-Roman culture as a symbol of the love of one's fellow human beings, as well as in Israel: he told the Apostles that they were shepherds (Matt. 9:35–10:16). The people were 'like sheep without a shepherd'; the Apostles were to go out to care for 'the lost sheep of the house of Israel'. His last instructions to Simon Peter were couched in 'shepherd' terms: 'Feed my sheep' (John 21:15–17). He drew upon the rich meaning of the same image to present his own mission (John 10). He was the Good Shepherd, who knew his own sheep and who had come to care for them and give them life. He would gather together sheep from other 'folds' than the one marked out by the Old Testament within which the Apostles had grown up, to bring them all into one flock, where they would recognize his voice and follow him.

When Our Lord spoke of giving his life for his followers, he referred to himself as the good shepherd who 'lays down his life for his sheep', not as the good priest. The good shepherd is one whose entire life has been dedicated to the care of his flock: everything he had done for them as well as the culmination in death itself. 'Listening to his voice', the sheep had come to know him and to trust in the loving care he had for them; the developed image is appropriate to the spoken character of revelation which we have already seen as fundamental to the New Covenant between God and humanity: there is always a living, personal exchange.

At the Last Supper, Christ clearly showed himself to be

CHRIST AND THE APOSTLES 81

the Good Shepherd by the gesture in which he expressed the giving of his life for his flock. The Passover was not a rite reserved to the official priests and confined to the Temple. It originated as a rite practised by shepherds, a family meal appropriate to nomads, preparing themselves to move on to their next place of pasture.[1] This was the context within which he set the consummation of his work, the feast that showed the significance of his death. The Apostles who were told to celebrate this feast in the same way, sharing now not the paschal lamb but the food and drink of his body and blood, were in consequence to think of themselves predominantly as shepherds, identified with the Good Shepherd from whom their calling and mission had come. Our Lord did not so much 'ordain his priests' at the Last Supper, as is often said, as confirm them graphically in their task as shepherds, showing himself to be the Good Shepherd (Ps. 23) by preparing a sacrificial banquet for them and for the flock which they were to feed on his behalf with the food he provided.

The Risen Christ continued to show that he wanted his Apostles to be fishermen and shepherds. In John 21 the 'fishing' context of the first calling of the Apostles reappears, and the pastoral command to 'Feed my sheep' is given. The author of the Epistle to the Hebrews prays, '... that the God of peace, who brought our Lord Jesus back from the dead to become the great Shepherd of the sheep by the blood that sealed an eternal covenant may make you ready to do his will in any kind of good action' (Heb. 13:20).

After Pentecost: Still Pastors

The use of the image of pastor continues in the first years of the Church to make the role of Christ's ministers clear. 'Pastors and teachers' are spoken of among those who have been

---

[1] R. de Vaux, *Ancient Israel*, 1961; 1973, 489.

82   A PEOPLE OF PRIESTS

given special gifts for building up the body of Christ (Eph.
4:11), and 'shepherd' is linked with *episcopos* (overseer,
bishop): Peter affirms that 'you have come back to the
shepherd and guardian [*episcopos*] of your souls' (1 Pet. 2:25).
The term that came into use to designate the chosen and
appointed leaders of the Christian communities is used here
in the same breath as the word 'shepherd'; Christ's choice of
metaphor is still applied in order to guide the thought of the
Church about the character of her leaders.

Farms and Vineyards

The writings of the apostolic period used other images drawn
by Our Lord from the work needed in the countryside to
secure food and other human necessities. The parables of
the sower, of the wicked husbandmen, of the workers in the
vineyard and of the vine all contribute to the self-understand-
ing of the Apostles.

> After all, what is Apollos and what is Paul? They are serv-
> ants who brought the faith to you. Even the different ways
> in which they brought it were assigned to them by the
> Lord. I did the planting, Apollos did the watering, but
> God made things grow. Neither the planter nor the waterer
> matters: only God, who makes things grow. It is all one
> who does the planting and who does the watering, and each
> will be duly paid according to his share in the work. We
> are fellow workers with God; you are God's farm, God's
> building. (1 Cor. 3:5–9)

Stewardship and Service

The use of parables drawn from stewardship and service in a
household prepared the way for Christ's full teaching about
service, given at the Last Supper, when he washed the Apos-

CHRIST AND THE APOSTLES 83

tles' feet, showing the way in which they were to carry out
their work (John 13:1–20).

Having heard Our Lord's warning about being ready for
the return of the Master, as good servants (at that return, it
is the Master who will serve those who have been faithful),
Peter asks to whom the parable applies (see Luke 12:35–48).
The Lord makes clear that it applies to all; but this is obviously particularly significant for the Apostles 'to whom a
great deal has been given': ' "What sort of steward, then, is
faithful and wise enough for the master to place him over his
household to give them their allowance of food at the proper
time?" ' (Luke 12:42). The servant comparison is also used
when our Lord evokes the image of the wedding feast to
describe the coming-in of the Kingdom and to indicate that
the Church will be the Bride of Christ. His followers are the
'bridegroom's attendants' who do not fast while he is with
them (Luke 5:33–5).

The professional virtues of servants were expected of all
Christ's followers, and thus particularly of those with special
responsibilities. The children of light were to be innocent,
yes, but they were also to be as competent, in their innocence,
as the crafty steward was in his deceitfulness (Luke 16:1–8).
Talents entrusted by a master to his servants were to be used
profitably (Luke 19:11–26).

Our Lord finally drew his Apostles into a closer relationship with himself than that of servants:

> 'I shall not call you servants any more,
> because a servant does not know
> his master's business;
> I call you friends,
> because I have made known to you
> everything I have learnt from my Father.'
> (John 15:14–15)

But that did not mean that they did not still have specific

84 A PEOPLE OF PRIESTS

tasks, that they were not still under obedience, that they were
not still expected to bear fruit, as the servants to whom talents
were given were expected to show profit:

> 'You are my friends,
> if you do what I command you . . .
> You did not choose me,
> no, I chose you;
> and I commissioned you
> to go out and to bear fruit,
> fruit that will last.' (John 15:14, 16)

This 'steward' (*oikonomos*) theme is essential for a comprehension of the Apostles' role, and of the work of all with
similar responsibility. Paul echoes Our Lord's words about
stewardship (Luke 12:35–48): 'People must think of us as
Christ's servants, stewards entrusted with the mysteries of
God. What is expected of stewards is that each one should
be found worthy of his trust' (1 Cor. 4:1–2).

The 'household' (*oikos* = house) image reminds the Apostles and other office-bearers that each one of them is responsible to a master who will require an account of his work, and
that the riches and goods they handle are not their own. They
are working for a family with all its members and dependents,
building up therefore a complete human community, held
together by its faith. For they are 'entrusted with the mysteries of God'; their service is the communication of those
mysteries, the means by which the family is created and
sustained.

1 Peter has the same theme and emphasis: 'Each one of
you has received a special grace, so like good stewards responsible for all these different graces of God, put yourselves
at the service of others' (4:10). And the Epistle to Titus
develops the 'steward' theme at length in its application to
the behaviour to be expected of a bishop: '. . . a bishop, as

CHRIST AND THE APOSTLES   85

God's steward [*oikonomos*][2] must be blameless; he must not
be arrogant or quick-tempered or a drunkard or violent or
greedy for gain, but hospitable, a lover of goodness, master
of himself, upright, holy and self-controlled' (Titus 1:7–8).
Pastoral responsibility and service on a farm and in a family
are thus found to provide appropriate ways of describing the
work of the Apostles. '. . . I have been entrusted by God with
the grace he meant for you . . . I have been made a servant of
that gospel by a gift of grace from God' (Eph. 3:2, 7), said St
Paul.

Slavery

Our Lord's own example went still further than the sign
he gave when he washed the Apostles' feet. Exhorting the
Philippians to unity and concord – 'always consider the other
person to be better than yourself' – Paul reminded them that
Christ, for their sakes, had become a slave: '. . . he did not
cling to his equality with God, but emptied himself to assume
the condition of a slave' (Phil. 2:5–8). The slavery accepted
by Christ was not a slavery of a social or economic kind. He
did not belong to someone else's household but was competent to live independently by his trade as a carpenter, learnt
in his own family. He took on the condition of a slave when
he underwent the punishment given to rebellious slaves. It
was death on the Cross that made him a slave in the eyes of
the world.

He accepted that status in order to win everyone for his
heavenly Father. He showed that the service he acknowledged, taught to others and practised himself was genuine
and complete, right to the end. The Lordship that he had
now been given, a Lordship that all must now acknowledge,
had been earned. He had done everything necessary to win

[2]The Jerusalem Bible has 'representative', which does not bring out the 'service
for the master of a household' significance of the term used.

the allegiance of us all (Phil. 2:9–11). In his Father's household, he had been the most faithful of servants and so had received the greatest of rewards.

Paul's teaching about service and his life of service followed the same pattern. Slaves had their own status, according to the dignity of the master whom they served. They could be members of important households, holding authority over others and acting as representatives of their masters in business and public affairs. Slavery to Christ means that he has bought us as slaves, bought us from another master. Slavery to Christ as master and patron means that he has conferred his status upon us, freeing us from all other bonds, from the imprisonment of sin and death. In our freedom, we are now able to use this world as we should use it, and can develop our talents as they should be developed. Loving God alone as our sole true master, we love all others, giving them their due, recognizing their rightful place in the household.

Slavery to Christ has given us our real status. We had been enslaved to ourselves and to the world in its alienation from God; from that slavery he has freed us, to be ourselves and so to give glory to God. This image illustrates in a particularly powerful way the reality of the change brought about by Christ and the striking novelty of titles given under the regime of the New Testament.

Paul applied the message of 'slavery to Christ so as to win true freedom' to the conduct of his ministry. As slave of Christ, he preached under compulsion. Christ had been given work to do, which he had completed, right to the end, and Paul was trying to do the same. Like Christ, Paul was 'not a slave of any man' (1 Cor. 9:19), but had accepted the slavery laid upon him by God. And that service, as Paul lived it, was worked out according to the implications of the standard set by Christ. Paul's pattern of life was not simply taken from that of the slave-steward of a wealthy family of the ancient world. He could have claimed the privileges of managerial

CHRIST AND THE APOSTLES　　87

status and still considered himself an adequate servant. He
could have earned his living by preaching the gospel, as the
Lord had directed, but he did not even do that. He made
himself 'the slave of everyone' (1 Cor. 9:19), in order that all
might find themselves at home in the Church, and in order
that the Church might live in peace and harmony, undamaged
in her inner life by the social distinctions and divisions of the
world.

He gave orders; he spoke with authority; but it was the
authority of one who spoke in the Church not as the representative of a particular group or interest, whether 'upper
class' or 'lower class', 'clerical' or 'lay', not as the defender
of any unchanging system which might benefit some at the
expense of others, but of one who spoke for Christ and who
in his Name sought to help everybody to find their true
place in the household of God.

Servants of the Word

When they wanted to sum up the work to which they had
been called, the thinking of the Apostles focussed especially
on the 'servant/slave' theme. And their work was service with
a particular priority. In sharing out their responsibilities
with others, they made quite clear what their principal task
was: ' "It would not be right for us to neglect the word of God
so as to give out food ['serve tables'] . . . [we will] continue to
devote ourselves to prayer and to the service of the word" '
(Acts 6:2–4). Everything else depended on their service of the
message they had to convey to the world. Important as it
was to serve people in their needs of every kind, the pastoral
service which they had to provide as Apostles was to represent Christ and to make him known. This was their overriding
concern (Acts 10:42; 13:44–7; St Paul, Rom. 1:1–2 and the
opening words of most of the epistles). It is Christ whom
they serve first; because they are his servants, they are com-

88 A PEOPLE OF PRIESTS

mitted to helping others in every possible way, but that help
is itself an act of witness, and the greatest help they can
bring is the knowledge and love of Christ.

St Paul on the Work of the Apostles

> People must think of us as Christ's servants, stewards
> entrusted with the mysteries of God. (1 Cor. 4:1)

> I became the servant of the Church when God made me
> responsible for delivering God's message to you, the
> message which was a mystery hidden for generations and
> centuries and has now been revealed to his saints. (Col.
> 1:25–6)

> I, who am less than the least of all the saints, have been
> entrusted with this special grace, not only of proclaiming
> to the pagans the infinite treasure of Christ, but also of
> explaining how the mystery is to be dispensed. (Eph. 3:8–9)

These three passages from St Paul confirm the priority set
by the Apostles in Acts 6. St Paul served God's purpose by
making that purpose known. The Gentiles were to be brought
to a knowledge of Christ, so that they might come to share
in what was their proper inheritance (Eph. 3:6).

It is the gospel that must be served, and served not just by
practising it, but by communicating it to others: it is to
be 'proclaimed' and 'explained'. God's purpose was to be
achieved, not independently of human cooperation, but
through Paul's involvement, with full awareness and understanding, in what he was called upon to do.

Paul uses the language of worship and of sacred duty when
speaking of this task of communicating the knowledge of
God: 'He has appointed me a minister [*leitourgos*] of Jesus
Christ, and I am to carry out my sacred duty [*hierourgounta*]

CHRIST AND THE APOSTLES 89

by bringing the good news from God to the pagans, and so make them acceptable as an offering, made holy by the Holy Spirit' (Rom. 15:16, my own translation; cf. Acts 26:16–18). His work as an Apostle, and the human fruits of his work, were the offering of a worshipping priest; his sacred duty consisted of communicating the gospel, and the effect of that communication was the transformation of the pagans, so that they in their turn were able to offer true worship. The context and purpose of his preaching is worship; his epistles open on this note (Rom. 1:8–9; 1 Cor. 1:4–5, 2 Cor. 1:3; Gal. 1:5; Eph. 1:3, etc.). And this worship is offered by the whole Church together – 'we are bold enough to approach God in complete confidence, through our faith in him' – because of the knowledge we now have of our part in the mystery of salvation (Eph. 3:1–2).

Within the priesthood of the whole Church, 'all grow into one holy temple in the Lord' (Eph. 2:21), and Paul's particular share in this worship, the work to which he had been called, was 'bringing the good news from God'. That was what made him the particular kind of priest that he was, and made him speak, with the other Apostles, of his personal offering as ambassadorship, as stewardship and the service of the Word.

The Mystery Is Christ Among You

Serving the Word means very much more than passing on useful information. Paul did not regard himself simply as an instructor, dealing in facts and guidelines designed to enlighten people's intellects and influence their behaviour. He relates all his activity to this one theme, the communication of the Word of God, precisely because the Word of God is Christ himself and all that he came to do. 'The mystery is Christ among you, your hope of glory; this is the Christ we proclaim, this is the wisdom in which we thoroughly train everyone and instruct everyone, to make them all perfect in Christ' (Col. 1:27–8; cf. Rom. 15:16, Eph. 3:7–9). The Word, mystery, wisdom: Paul is speaking of the plan of God for our salvation, once hidden from human knowledge, but progressively made known and now in Christ revealed to us so that we may consciously and willingly take our part within it. The Word means action as well as knowledge; God expresses himself in events and persons which embody his purpose and reveal his nature to us.

Paul sees himself as a servant of this divine plan. He tells the members of the Church at Colossae that Christ is acting amongst them, giving them their motive for living, their 'hope of glory'. Christ has chosen and sent his apostle to help those who have heard the message and believed it to understand and to respond. They are to be trained in wisdom, being changed by it at the same time as they begin to act in terms of what they have learnt. Their 'being made perfect in Christ' is the aim of Paul's work, as he also says in the letter to the Romans (15:16).

Paul cooperates with God's purpose in history by enabling others to play their part in that purpose, and so to fulfil their destiny. As a priest, he offers to God the lives of those whom he has helped by making them capable of being priests in their turn and in their own distinctive way. That is why he speaks of 'the God I worship spiritually by preaching the Good News of his Son' (Rom. 1:9); preaching is an act of worship by which, as God's fisherman and God's shepherd, he gathers those to whom he speaks into the Church of God.

His understanding of his role as servant of the mystery, made explicit in the passage just quoted from Colossians, underlies all his exhortations and words of encouragement. Speaking to the Philippians, he says, 'It is God, for his own loving purpose, who puts both the will and the action in you' (2:13), and refers to their 'own sacrifice and offering – which is your faith' (2:17). Preaching the Word of God always has

CHRIST AND THE APOSTLES 91

this sacerdotal purpose, that by taking part willingly and actively in God's plan for them, believers may offer themselves as a holy sacrifice to God. They are priests – they offer sacrifice – and so is Paul, in serving the Word and his hearers.

Paul clearly thinks of preaching as much more than giving a lesson. The Word of whom he speaks, speaks through him. The Word is a dynamic reality, which has its own power to grow and bear fruit. The image of growth and cultivation which he uses (1 Cor. 3:6) relates to the parable of the sower. The message of Christ has its own inherent life.

Luke expressed this in the Acts of the Apostles through references to the regular growth of the Word of God (6:7; 12:24; 13:49; 19:20). Speaking of the numerical expansion of the Church, he says that it is the 'Word of God' that is growing and spreading. In the explanation of the parable of the sower given in his Gospel, he makes particular use of this theme: 'the seed is the word of God' (Luke 8:11). So the Word is alive; it can be identified with the Church in which it is embodied, and which grows in a verifiable and quantifiable way.

Speaking and Hearing the Word

This power of life is to be found particularly in the spoken word. The fact that Jesus taught by word of mouth is emphasized in Matthew's Gospel at the beginning of the Sermon on the Mount: 'He opened his mouth and taught them, saying . . .' (5:2). This statement of what may appear to be the obvious is nevertheless particularly significant. Oral/aural communication establishes a link between speaker and hearer, and so is appropriate as the means that brings the New Testament Church into being. Spoken words cannot be detached from the persons who speak them. To 'hear the

92 A PEOPLE OF PRIESTS

word and keep it' (Luke 11:28) is to be drawn into an association, a friendship, with the one from whom one hears it.

Christ declared that his family is made up of those 'who hear the word of God and put it into practice' (Luke 8:19–21). Speaking and listening to one another leads to the establishment of the strongest of personal bonds. He can only compare the relationship that is established with the biological relationship that exists between fathers, mothers and children; and since that relationship has to be broken if we are to be his true followers, and then remade through faith in him, he is clearly saying that belief in the Word gives rise to an even stronger bond. The act of faith, calling upon the exercise of our intelligence and our will, and expressed in spoken words, brings into being a more enduring relationship than that resulting from genetic inheritance.

Christ chose to spread his message by word of mouth through those who acknowledged him as the Incarnate Word of God, because it is the most effective method of communication. Human beings need to relate to other human beings. We use writing and print as a support in our search for knowledge, but it is the human voice, the human person, that we need for real communication. That is why 'the Word of God' is so profoundly significant as a title of Christ: he does not simply bring God's words, he is himself God's Word, spoken to us, face to face, so that we may hear and reply. And that is why 'Servants of the Word' is the most expressive title of the Apostles and of the bishops, presbyters and deacons who succeed them.

Images That Were Not Used: Prophet, Priest and King

Christ did not in his teaching establish a link between the Apostles and the public functionaries of the Old Testament, prophet, priest and king. The traditional roles of these guides

CHRIST AND THE APOSTLES 93

and rulers of Israel were under the New Testament drawn together and exercised by Christ himself, as a single living synthesis in his own person. The titles thus become applicable to all who 'in Christ' are members of his Body, whether ordained or not.

The Second Vatican Council used these categories to provide a threefold classification of the work of Christ and of his ordained representatives (*L.G.* nn. 20, 25–8, 34–6; *C.D.* n. 11; *P.O.* nn. 1, 4). The three functions were certainly spoken of and expounded by the New Testament writers, the Fathers and the Scholastics, but the titles were not so systematically grouped together. Reference to the threefold office came into theology through John Calvin and was taken up by Lutheran scholars in the seventeenth century. Catholic theologians began to use the theme of the threefold office at the end of the eighteenth century.

The three titles, used in this way, certainly enabled the Council to provide a broader and more inclusive doctrine of the ordained ministry, and particularly of the presbyterate, than that which since the Middle Ages was governed by the two categories of Order and Jurisdiction, or which, since Trent, has concentrated on the Eucharist and on the sacerdotal theme. We should however beware of accepting them as the only way or as necessarily the best way of understanding the work of Christ and of his Apostles and their successors in this ministry.

The threefold division endangers our view of the unity and the originality of the new role that Our Lord conferred on the Apostles and on those with whom they were to share their ministry. Further, we may all too easily retain an Old Testament or even pagan interpretation of these social functions, and thus unwittingly confine within a pre-Christian mode those who should be playing their part in the style of the New Testament.

And once the classification has been made and spelt out, it

94 A PEOPLE OF PRIESTS

is possible, also, to opt for one group of characteristics and tasks rather than another: particularly, perhaps, to concentrate on the sacerdotal role while neglecting the others.

The use of this triple sub-division, its source, its usefulness, its dangers, certainly needs further investigation (see also Chapter 4, p. 112). But in the search for what it is to be an Apostle and thus an ordained minister of the Church, one must first of all and above all look at the images Our Lord himself used to make clear the calling he had in mind; and these did not include prophet, priest or king.

Going back beyond these social categories to an earlier stage in human history and to more fundamental and widespread human activities, Christ used the work of the pastor-nomad and of the hunter-fisherman, together with that of the farmer, employing images of settled cultivation, the harvest of corn and the harvest of wine, and spoke of stewardship and service in the household and at the wedding feast, when he wished to illustrate the way in which he would be represented.

And the Apostles spoke in the same way about themselves and their fellow pastors:

> Tend the flock of God that is in your charge, not by constraint but willingly, not for shameful gain but eagerly, not as domineering over those who are in your charge, but being examples to the flock. And when the chief Shepherd is manifested, you will obtain the unfading crown of glory. (1 Pet. 5:2–4)

The shepherd image, used by Christ in his final injunction to Peter, is clearly still in the forefront of Peter's mind, judging by the instructions he gave to his 'fellow elders' (*sumpresbuteroi*); it is the best characterization of the work they have to do as elders responsible for the Church of God.

Paul uses the same term in his farewell words to the elders (*presbuteroi*) of Ephesus:

CHRIST AND THE APOSTLES 95

Be on your guard for yourselves and for all the flock of which the Holy Spirit has made you the overseers [*episcopoi*], to feed [note: as shepherds, *poimainein*; *poimen* is a shepherd] the Church of God which he bought with his own blood. I know quite well that when I have gone fierce wolves will invade you and will have no mercy on the flock. (Acts 20:28–9)

It is the word 'shepherd' that comes to mind when those who look after the Church (*episcopoi*, *presbuteroi*) are to be encouraged and exhorted.

4

Bishops, Presbyters and Deacons

The Apostolic Community

Christ deliberately conveyed his message to the world of his own time and to the generations that would follow by means of the community he created. The faith of the disciples was given a social expression in new relationships with each other and with those to whom they were sent. His teaching took root and began to grow, not just in the lives of disparate individuals, for the enrichment of their private life, but in a people. To the world around them, they were the visible sign of his influence: a body of followers who practised what he preached and who by their existence showed that the People of God had now moved into the last stage of their journey. The promises of the Old Testament had been fulfilled and a new People had been sent out to draw in all the nations of the earth.

And he gave that community a definite structure; by retaining that structure, the community would remain recognizably the same. Persisting through time and across the world with the identical pattern of life, they would provide living evidence of his power and continuing presence. The Apostles shared with him a common life in the midst of the wider community of his disciples and of the many others who followed him, out of curiosity or out of some degree of commitment. And they knew themselves to be responsible

BISHOPS, PRESBYTERS AND DEACONS

for reproducing that common life in the families of believers that sprang up wherever the gospel was preached.

The very first community brought into being by the Apostles had all the marks of what the Church was then and still remains. After Peter's preaching at Pentecost, 'That very day about three thousand were added to their number. These remained faithful to the teaching of the apostles, to the brotherhood, to the breaking of bread and to the prayers' (Acts 2:41–2). 'The teaching of the apostles': that comes first, as the means that called the community together and then enabled them to persevere in unity. One might have expected an affirmation of their loyalty to 'the teaching of Christ', but instead we have 'the teaching of the apostles'. They believed, not just what Christ alone had said, as if he had been a solitary teacher, but the joint witness of those who were able to give a personal account of his actions and the events of his life as well as pass on what they had heard him say. Christ entrusted the success of his mission entirely to his Apostles; from the beginning to the end of his public life, he associated with himself an organized body of witnesses who would bear out the truth of what he said by their own response to him.

'The Teaching of the Apostles': in one form or another, that is the title of many early documents summing up the Christian message and life, from 'The Acts of the Apostles' onwards: the Apostles' Creed, the *Didache* or *The Teaching of the Twelve Apostles* and *The Apostolic Constitutions* are examples.

The bond between Christ and his Apostles will always be part of the Christian way of thinking, so familiar as to be taken for granted and perhaps unappreciated until some crisis reminds us of Christ's undying attachment to his Church and to those whom he chooses to care for it.

> Christ's law and his apostles twelve
> He taught, and first he followed it himself

wrote Geoffrey Chaucer of his 'poor Parson'; the fifteenth century, unconsciously perhaps, echoes the first.

Next, the brotherhood, the fellowship, the communion, the *koinonia*: those who respond in faith to the proclamation of the teaching are drawn into a united community. This will always be the true order of priorities. The Church will be held together by her faith in the gospel, and the prime task of her pastors will be to retain a hold on that faith, passing judgement on controversies that threaten the unity of the Church or on rival teachings that lead Christians away on other paths. And that unity of faith will not be limited to intellectual agreement, to being of one mind; it will be expressed in the practical concern of the brethren for one another and in the care of the poor.

'The breaking of bread' is the third feature of the community to be mentioned: the expression in worship of their common life, the sign given to them by Christ at the Last Supper as the means of maintaining their union with him, present among them, and with one another.

Finally, 'the prayers'; the life of the community, both corporate and individual, is a constant conversation with God. They are not alone; they are not serving an absent master, but one who has undertaken to be with them always. Praise and thanksgiving run through the Acts of the Apostles and the writings of St Paul; they are the natural, unselfconscious expression of those who have come to believe in Christ.

Pastoral Care in the Next Generation

The Apostles saw themselves as responsible for building communities of this kind and ensuring their continuing life. Their work to this end was a ministry, a service, a *diakonia* (Acts 1:17, 25; 20:24; Rom. 11:3), for which they had been chosen and given authority, and it was to be shared with others in

BISHOPS, PRESBYTERS AND DEACONS

order that the life engendered by the gospel could spread and continue. They appointed elders (*presbuteroi*) for the churches (Acts 14:23) who with them took action to protect good order and unity (Acts 15:2, 4, 6, 22, 23). When addressing the presbyters, exhorting them to tend the flock as good shepherds, in expectation of the reward to be given by the chief Shepherd, Peter speaks of himself as a 'fellow presbyter' (1 Pet. 5:1). The presbyters are also referred to as *episcopoi*, overseers, bishops, with the same pastoral imagery being applied to the duty laid upon them (Acts 20:28).

In the First Epistle to Timothy (3:1–13), the virtues, experience and practical managing ability required in those chosen to be an *episcopos* or a *diaconos* are set out in detail. These particular names are specially used for those who hold responsibility for the life of the community as a whole, old and young, rich and poor, a general responsibility on the same lines as that which was laid upon the Apostles. By the turn of the first century, the writings of Clement of Rome and Ignatius of Antioch show that the roles of bishop, presbyter and deacon in ensuring the good conduct of church life were now taken for granted. Bishops and presbyters preside over Christian communities; deacons help them, without having the same overall authority.

All three functionaries look back to the Apostles as having originated and exercised their roles in the first place. The Apostles had been concerned with the witness to Christ by their preaching that called the churches into existence; they had appointed presbyters to help them in their work, sharing their authority with them and speaking of themselves as 'fellow presbyters'; and they had appointed others as their assistants without the same presidential authority, to whom the title of *diakonos*, also used by the Apostles of themselves, had been given.

Bishops, presbyters, deacons: the Apostles were all three. They exercised oversight, they identified themselves with the presbyters, they regarded themselves as deacons. The overlapping of vocabulary at the beginning is a normal consequence of the initial exercise of these functions by the same group of persons. The shared pastoral care exercised by bishops, presbyters and deacons, now separated out from the original apostolic nucleus, and the pattern of relationships between them, which had become settled by the end of the first century, is a continuation of the cellular pattern of life and of relationships that existed in the case of Christ with the Apostles and then of Peter with the other Apostles. One presides, to bring about unity, in a ministry that he shares with others, to bring about community. That people called deacons should be part of this apostolic and pastoral group provides a constant practical reminder of the fact that all are servants, in their own distinctive ways.

This presentation makes 'bishop' the equivalent of *episcopos*. It is sometimes suggested that the *episcopos* of the New Testament was not yet the 'bishop' as he came to be understood, and as we understand him now. But 'bishop' is simply the same word as *episcopos* in its modern English form. Reluctance to use the word now for *episcopos* presumably arises from the associations the word has acquired over the centuries, from thoughts of prince-bishops, of prelacy and of what in 1 Peter is called 'domineering' or 'being a dictator' (5:3). Misuse of the office should always be resisted in the name of the original intention; but the office itself and its name need to be retained, being continually corrected and given new inspiration through confrontation with the New Testament reality. That is where the meaning is to be found, and that is where we must return in order to stay on the right path.

The documents make quite clear the fact that the Apostles were specially chosen and given their particular mission by Christ himself. *Mutatis mutandis*, one can say the same of those to whom they passed on their ministry: by the public

BISHOPS, PRESBYTERS AND DEACONS 101

act of the laying-on of hands, bishops, presbyters and deacons were formally given their office in the Church as a responsibility laid on them by God (Acts 6:2; 13:3; 2 Tim 1:6). The authority they were able to claim depended entirely on the fact that they were God's representatives, building up and guiding the Church on his behalf.

That this was a distinctive function belonging exclusively to certain individuals, is shown by the fact that these titles were not used in a general sense, as 'priest' or 'apostle', for example, have been used, since in Christ all are priests, and all share in the apostolic mission in one way or another. The special ministry allotted to the Apostles in the first place for teaching, governing and guiding the Church was passed on to particular individuals, who were given particular titles. Bishops, presbyters and deacons have work to do which is distinct, 'essentially different', from the work given to others. If this were not so, the 'Order' which is their concern and by which they are identified in the list of sacraments of the Church, would be frustrated, and, indeed, unattainable. In their persons, each one individually and together as a group, they are the gathering-point, the centre of unity for each Christian community.

The recognition and confirmation of the fact that they are God's choice for this service (irrespective of the methods of selection that have been used, which can and do vary) is expressed by the laying-on of hands. Just as baptism makes us once and for all members of the Church, so this ordination, for the growth and unity of the Church, constitutes an act by which God commits himself definitively to the work of our salvation.

The permanent character of the granting of this ministry is an illustration of the Church's faith in the reliability of God's word, and of our acknowledgement of his sovereign initiative in our lives. These are not tasks taken up as voluntary service and laid down at some later date according to personal choice.

102 A PEOPLE OF PRIESTS

To be bishop, presbyter or deacon rests on God's choice, recognized by the individual and by the Church, not on our own inclination. Bishops, presbyters and deacons are part of the living, recognizable fabric of the Church that God is building. Freedom enters in when we exercise personal choices over the manner and the detailed action whereby we respond to our calling, but the fact of the call is not ours to create or to deny (cf. pp. 91–2 on the stable, permanent character of the action of the Word).

The Pattern Continues

When we come to the end of the first century, the language used of public office in the Church in the principal documents of the time, 1 Clement and the letters of St Ignatius of Antioch, is more settled than it is in the New Testament documents, but there is no doubt of the continuity of the principle involved.

> The Apostles received the Gospel for us from the Lord Jesus Christ. Jesus Christ was sent from God. Christ therefore is from God and the Apostles from Christ. . . . They preached from district to district, and from city to city, and they appointed their first converts, testing them by the Spirit, to be bishops and deacons of the future believers. (1 Clement XLII)

The fluidity of vocabulary – 'bishops and deacons' here, without mention of 'presbyters'; elsewhere, 'presbyters' without mention of 'bishops' – has made possible much ecclesiastical polemic over the centuries. It would be a mistake to pin the Church down to one moment in the ordering of these relationships; such structures are necessarily conditioned to some extent by the circumstances of the time and need to be adapted when circumstances change. It is sufficient to stick to

BISHOPS, PRESBYTERS AND DEACONS 103

the essential reality, discoverable throughout Church history from the beginning: a corporate body centred on an individual with overall responsibility, who comes to be called 'the bishop', and made up of presbyters and deacons who are his fellow-workers in the service they all give to the Church. The relative importance of the parts played by the members of this group has fluctuated throughout history; for the good of the Church, they need constantly to be reminded of the gospel pattern.

An Authentic Ministry of the New Testament?

Both Clement and Ignatius are concerned that the churches should be faithfully obedient to those who have been given pastoral responsibility over them. In support of their instructions, they use illustrations drawn from the Old Testament and establish parallels between bishops, presbyters and deacons and the divine Persons, as well as the Apostles. Does this mean that they are using the Old Testament in such a way as to promote a return to the Aaronic priesthood, losing sight of the originality of the New Testament? Or that they are creating a pattern of ministry owing more to Greek thought about symbols and reality than to historic facts?

It would be a mistake to read the comparisons they use in this way, and to draw the conclusion that corruption of the gospel provision had already set in. One must look at the main thrust of their arguments.

Clement is above all concerned for good order and harmony in the Church. The authority of the duly appointed presbyters in Corinth had been challenged and indeed overthrown. His whole letter is directed towards the restoration of the previous peace in the community, now grievously shattered. In his exhortation, he uses examples drawn from the world of nature and from the army as well as from the Old

Testament in order to show how the Church should live in peace, with respect and concern for all her members:

> Let, therefore, our whole body be preserved in Christ Jesus, and let each be subject to his neighbour, according to the position granted to him. Let the strong care for the weak and let the weak reverence the strong. Let the rich man bestow help on the poor and let the poor give thanks to God, that he gave him one to supply his needs ... (1 Clem. XXXVIII)

Clement was using all the examples he could think of (including ones drawn from the cosmos, LV) in order to impress on the people of the Church in Corinth their duty to restore good order. He was not advocating a return to the Old Testament which would bring back the old priesthood within the new People of God.

The Old Testament provided him with examples of good order from the past, but the order that he was now trying to establish was that of the Church of the New Testament as Christ had made it:

> Now may God, the all-seeing, and the master of spirits, and the Lord of all flesh, who chose out the Lord Jesus Christ, and us through him for 'a peculiar people', give unto every soul that is called after his glorious and holy name, faith, fear, peace, patience and long-suffering, self-control, purity, sobriety, that they may be well-pleasing to his name through our high priest and guardian Jesus Christ, through whom be to him glory and majesty, might and honour, both now and to all eternity. Amen. (1 Clem. LXIV)

The letters of Ignatius to the Asian Churches are similarly concerned with the preservation of order:

> ... it is fitting that you should live in harmony with the will of the bishop, as indeed you do. For your justly famous

BISHOPS, PRESBYTERS AND DEACONS

presbytery, worthy of God, is attuned to the bishop as the strings to a harp. (To the Ephesians, IV)

The comparisons that he uses to support his case – for example, 'it is clear that we must regard the bishop as the Lord himself' – have given rise to the idea that we are now seeing the emergence of an ecclesiology based on Platonic symbolism, with earthly realities being seen as the projected shadows or images of the realities of heaven, and historical fact being undervalued. Whatever the rights, wrongs and limitations of the use of Platonic categories to interpret the mystery of faith and the life of the Church, such as developed later, one cannot say that Ignatius put more weight on Platonism than on revelation. The parallels he uses are not fixed or systematic; he says, for example, that the bishop is to be respected 'as the Lord himself', but he also says 'according to the power of God the Father' (Magnesians III).

He also says: '. . . let all respect the deacon as Jesus Christ, even as the bishop is also a type of the Father, and the presbyters as the council of God and the college of Apostles. Without these the name of "Church" is not given' (Trallians III; cf. Magnesians VI). But elsewhere he uses another analogy: 'Wherever the bishop appears let the congregation be present; just as wherever Jesus Christ is there is the Catholic Church' (Smyrnaeans VIII). Both deacon and bishop are seen as representing Christ. Ignatius is talking about attitudes, authority and behaviour, not about an artificial construction built on lines imported from philosophy; his source and justification is the unified pattern of life inherited from the Apostles.

Ordination – the sacrament of Order – is to be understood as the special gift of the Spirit which brings concord and harmony into the immense variety that exists in the worshipping Body of Christ. Although at different periods of history other interpretations have prevailed, and the clergy have been

106   A PEOPLE OF PRIESTS

seen as members of an *ordo clericorum*, alongside the orders
of the knights and of the *humiles*, the lesser mortals, or as
constituting a particular estate of the realm, these are cultural
developments temporarily overlaying the essential reality,
which requires that the successors of the Apostles, the bishops, presbyters and deacons, should for the sake of unity and
peace in the whole Body of Christ avoid allowing themselves
to be socially categorized in this way. Clement and Ignatius
were talking about a new pattern of ministry, which would
create a new type of society. They were not commending the
social system of either the Old Testament or the Empire, but
the communion of the Church.

A Special Gift: a Sacrament

This group of servants of the gospel and hence of the Church
has come to be recognized as constituting a sign that conveys
a special gift to the world. They hold an office the character
of which reveals God's care for us and carries out his purpose
for us in his Church. Since it depends upon the initiative of
God in calling those to whom the office is given, it has been
classified with other similar gifts as a sacrament in the strict
sense of the word. Other gifts of God do not have the same
permanence or general application, being given only to one
person, perhaps, or for one particular time and place; here
we have a reality that is part of the perennial life of the
Church, the presence of which always makes the Church
recognizable as the Church of Christ and the Apostles.

The Second Vatican Council has enabled us to see this
sacrament, designed to create community, as itself a community. Bishop, presbyters and deacons, together in one diocese, are a living specimen, so to speak, a single expression of
this sacrament. After centuries of debate among theologians,
the Council has established that the bishop is to be under-

BISHOPS, PRESBYTERS AND DEACONS   107

stood as having received the sacrament in its fullness, and therefore as being responsible for giving it through his ministry and life a complete expression; he gathers the whole group of ordained ministers together and leads them in their pastoral role. Without the presbyters and deacons the significance of this sacrament would not be visibly expressed. They share with him to different degrees the corporate responsibility they have together been given for the whole Church.

A theology that argued from the fact that the presbyter celebrates the Eucharist, the highest act of worship of the Church, and therefore must be said to have the fullness of the sacrament, found it difficult to see what was added, so to speak, when he was made a bishop, apart from the power of jurisdiction within the government of the Church. A theology that puts in the first place the pastoral responsibility that is conferred, and the service of the Word that is its prime means of operation, enables us to see the work of the bishop and of the presbyters and deacons who work with him in a much more complete and unified way, with due weight given to every aspect of their ministry (*L.G.* nn. 21, 28, 29).

This sacramental body derives its character entirely from its origin in the College of the Apostles. Its members are all representatives sent by God to speak and act on his behalf. Their authority depends entirely on this: not on their personal qualities, their talents, their experience, their venerability, but on God's choice. For that reason, they speak to our faith. They are witnesses to whom we give our credence, or from whom we withhold it: '. . . you will be my witnesses not only in Jerusalem but throughout Judaea and Samaria, and indeed to the ends of the earth' (Acts 1:8). Before they are anything else, they are people whose word we believe. Obedience follows on trust: trust in Christ whose word we acknowledge as true, and therefore trust in those whom he has sent to represent him. They have no power other than the delegation they have received, and no authority to speak other than to deliver the message with which they have been entrusted. Obedience to them in the administration of the Church is never 'blind', because it is exercised within our continuing act of faith in people whom we know, an act of our intelligence and free will.

The duty of the bishops to continue the work of the Apostles by safeguarding and communicating the faith has been regularly enough retained in the awareness of the Church throughout her history. But the full significance of that transmitted responsibility has not always been brought out in practice. It means that their prime concern, affirmed by Trent and by Vatican II, is to assure themselves and others of the authenticity and reliability of what they are teaching and for embodying this teaching in believing communities, bound together by love of the one Lord. Their rule and administration are guided by the practice of the Apostles, not by 'the kings of the earth'. As well as being pastors of their own diocese, they have corporate responsibility for the transmission of the message world-wide. The two horizons, local and universal, have to be kept in view; universal, in order to prevent nationalism from usurping the rights of the Kingdom of God, and local, in order to give the gospel a real human expression, on a human scale.

The share in this apostolic function given to presbyters and deacons has not always been so clearly seen, either in practice or in theory. But since the oversight of the individual Christian communities that go to make up a unit of the Church – a diocese – in a particular place is shared individually and corporately by the presbyters in communion with their bishop, the means used to build that community are the same: by teaching and example, to convince people of the truth of the gospel. When St Paul described himself as an ambassador for Christ (2 Cor. 5:20; an ambassador 'in chains': Eph. 6:20), he was using a verb (*presbeuo*) that expressed his apostolic status and shed some light by association on the share given

BISHOPS, PRESBYTERS AND DEACONS 109

to presbyters in the work of the Apostles and those who succeeded them.

'Deacon' (*diakonos*) also denotes a share in that work. A recent comprehensive study of both pagan and Christian usage has enlarged our understanding of *diakonia* by showing that it is a service given as a representative, an emissary, a spokesman, an ambassador sent to convey a message.[1] The standing of the deacon, like that of the apostle, derives from the status of the one whom he represents. This indicates that the share given to 'the Seven' by the Apostles in Acts 6, while it was clearly a recruitment of others to help with the material side of the Apostles' work for the community, was nevertheless also a share in their responsibility for witness to the gospel message, as the later preaching of Stephen emphatically makes plain. While they do not have overall guardianship of the Word and charge of the life of the community (and hence do not preside at the Eucharist or administer the sacrament of reconciliation), they are, with the bishop and presbyter, and under their guidance and leadership, commissioned for preaching the gospel as members of the sacramental group that continues the work of the Apostles.

That 'Essential Difference'

When we come to define this group, what is the characteristic image set before us by the Council? It is that of pastor, shepherd. This was expounded in one of the most solemn statements of *Lumen Gentium*, one of the two documents that has the status of a Dogmatic Constitution:

> This most sacred Synod, following in the footsteps of the First Vatican Council, teaches and declares with that Coun-

---

[1]Collins, John N., *Diakonia*. Re-interpreting the Ancient Sources, OUP, 1990.

cil that Jesus Christ, the eternal Shepherd, established his holy Church by sending forth the Apostles as he himself had been sent by the Father (cf. John 20:21). He willed that their successors, namely the bishops, should be shepherds in his Church even to the consummation of the world. (*L. G.* 18)

It is round that theme, studied in Chapter 3, that the whole ministry and life of bishops, and hence of presbyters and deacons, should be organized. The shepherd image gives the bishops their clear identity:

... with their helpers, the presbyters and deacons, [they] have taken up the service of the community, presiding in the place of God over the flock whose shepherds they are ...

... this sacred synod teaches that by divine institution bishops have succeeded to the place of the apostles as shepherds of the Church, and that he who hears them hears Christ, while he who rejects them, rejects Christ and him who sent Christ. (Luke 10:16) (n. 20)

This is what marks off the bishops and so also the presbyters and deacons who are united with them and work with them for the pastoral care of the Church. Within the Body of Christ, within the priesthood of all the faithful, conferred by baptism, which they still share, the worship they offer is the special service of the shepherds of the flock, which they and they alone, for the benefit of all, are called and ordained to exercise. The unity of each cell of the Church is expressed and safeguarded by the one bishop who is its pastor, together with those who are ordained to share in the same service. The pastorate, for the one community, is itself a united community.

Since the bishop is above all the pastor, and holds the fullness of the sacrament of order, those who share that sacramental role will be pastors too. The union of presbyters with

BISHOPS, PRESBYTERS AND DEACONS 111

their bishop in the care of their part of the Church is spoken of in strongly pastoral terms in the conciliar decree *Christus Dominus*, on the Pastoral Office of Bishops in the Church (nn. 28ff.):

> In exercising this care of souls, pastors and their assistants should so fulfil their duty of teaching, sanctifying and governing that the individual parishioners and the parish communities will really feel that they are members of the diocese and of the universal Church. (n. 30.1)

> In fulfilling the office of shepherd, pastors should first take pains to know their own flock. (n. 30.2)

What is said here explicitly of diocesan clergy is applied also to members of religious orders:

> Religious priests are consecrated for the office of the presbyterate so that they may be the prudent cooperators of the episcopal order. (n. 34)

'Pastor' should not of course be confined to being a technical term for those who are working as parish priests and their assistants. What is here stated in the precise terms of the language of canon law should read in the light of the deeper insight of the Council, which sees 'pastor' as the title that unifies and characterizes the work that every ordained minister is in one way or another called to offer as his priestly worship to God.

Episcopate, presbyterate, diaconate: each is a single ministry, *ministerium*, with a number of duties, *munera* (*L.G.* nn. 24, 25). The role of pastor integrates for the ordained ministry the three duties of teaching, worshipping and governing – prophet, priest and king – which were inherited from the Old Testament, were drawn into a single synthesis by Christ himself, the Good Shepherd, and are now shared by all the faithful, each in a particular and distinctive way. As we have

112 A PEOPLE OF PRIESTS

seen (Chapter 3, pp. 92–5), the three titles were not applied directly or in any exclusive sense to the Apostles or to those who followed them in the New Testament, but were used generally of the whole Body of Christ. Within the Body, the ordained minister's way of being prophet, priest and king, his *ministerium, métier*, trade, competence, is responsibility for building up and looking after Christ's People: for being their publicly authorized and recognizable leader and guide.

Recent studies have emphasized the fact that these functions of prophet, priest and king must always be given their due expression and exercised together in the work of the pastor. If any one of them is allowed to predominate and to substitute itself for the one overarching and unifying function of shepherd, sent by Christ as his representative, then witness to the faith is impoverished and the faith-community suffers.[2]

Herein, then, lies the unity of this sacrament of service and that 'essential difference' that marks it off within the priesthood of Christ and his Church. It is not that bishops, presbyters and deacons are priests, while the others are not. It is not that they are priests in some more intense way, or bigger, more elevated or better priests, for the difference is not one of degree. They do not receive a simple reinforcement of baptism, but a separate and distinct gift, by which they are made priests of a special kind. Their own particular priestly worship, their contribution to the sacrifice of praise offered

---

[2]Yves Congar OP, 'Sur la trilogie, Prophète – Roi – Prêtre', *Revue des Sciences Philosophiques et Théologiques*, 67, 1983, 97–115: '(the three functions) are certainly to be distinguished, in order, however, to unite them in what, following Scripture, we will call the pastorate ... the Second Vatican Council had a lively awareness of the unity of the pastoral ministry'.

Henri de Lubac SJ, *Théologie dans l'Histoire*. 1. La Lumière du Christ, Paris, 1991, 26 n. 16: 'If we dissolved the synthesis and divided the ministerium into separate bits, we would have great difficulty in avoiding, all at the same time or one after the other, according to current trends, legalism in government, academicism in teaching and superstition in worship'.

BISHOPS, PRESBYTERS AND DEACONS   113

by the Church, is the service of the Church as her pastors, feeding the flock with the Word of God.

This is indeed the *summum sacerdotium*, the *sacri ministerii summa* (*L.G.* n. 21), because it is the principal service that can be offered, the summing-up of all service; but it is that not in contradistinction from the rest of the Church but within the priesthood of the whole Church, to serve it as provider and leader. It is different, radically different, essentially different, simply because that is the way in which the unity of the Church in every place and in its world-wide extent can be assured. For each community there can only be one pastor-bishop, united with his presbyters and deacons, to call together, to preserve and to foster the united expression of its single symphony, its harmony of praise.

The Future of the Ordained Ministry: Source, Selection and Training

The present decline in vocations in Western Europe and in the United States, and the strains felt by those who have been ordained, to the extent of numerous departures, are in part the result of assigning to priests an inadequate social rôle. As long as they are seen as above all the custodians and administrators of the sacraments within a society that has retained a traditional Catholic faith and allots them a definite, recognized function, and as long as they maintain the function given to them, together with a way of living and acting that sets them strictly apart, their identity is clear. When society as a whole no longer believes, they are left without a clear purpose; no one wants the service they have to offer.

Recovery will come in the first place not by an attempt to restore the ritual-based image of the ordained ministry, but through a renewed conviction of the significance of the person of Jesus Christ in human history, and consequently

114 A PEOPLE OF PRIESTS

of the representatives he has chosen and sent out to continue his work. The identity of the clergy does not derive from the world, nor yet from unexamined tradition, but from the person of Christ, who in new circumstances always has new ways to teach us. Vocations can only be fostered and ordained ministers properly trained through a fresh grasp of the truth of the Christian message: the historic truth of Christian origins and the relevance for human life of what Christ has taught us.

And in the second place, it will come if bishops, presbyters and deacons strengthen their understanding of themselves as people sent by God to build up believing communities. Their responsibility will primarily be one of persuading people of the value and reliability of the gospel. They cannot take for granted a pre-existing community into which they will fit and in which they will simply have to carry out duties long standardized and prescribed.[3]

In other words, they will have the responsibility of building from scratch, of bringing the Church into being where she does not exist, which will test their capabilities to the utmost. They will need qualities of leadership and management, of teaching and counselling as great as those demanded in any human enterprise. Their suitability for ordination must be judged in part by these human qualities; it is not enough that they are pious and obedient, which may simply mean that

---

[3]'First of all, we must focus all our strength on the authenticity of a life of faith. This means that in the parish we must form living cells and bring people together to reflect and ask themselves how they can live out the Scriptures. In this, the priest will play, more than before, the rôle of a spiritual partner. . . . In such a community, the priest would be the shepherd who focuses his whole strength on proclaiming the word of God; who discovers charisma and capacity for reciprocal service; who initiates faith experiences; who spiritually assists people who are searching; and who upholds the relationship with the bishop and the successor of Peter.' *On Being Priests in the Modern World*, Message by the Episcopal Conference of Germany, in *Catholic International*, IV, 7, (1993), 332–7.

BISHOPS, PRESBYTERS AND DEACONS 115

they are lacking in initiative and determination. They must be chosen on a basis of real achievement. They must be respected and accepted by the community as capable of instructing them in the faith, leading them in worship and guiding them in service to one another and to the community at large.

This means that there should be many roads to ordination as well as the road through the seminary for young men where they receive education in the faith, spiritual formation and a practical initiation into pastoral work. Candidates for ordination should be sought in the general priestly body of the Church, among older men who prove themselves by their practice of the Christian faith to be appropriate leaders and servants of the community.

This means a reconsideration of the idea that the ministry of the Church is almost exclusively recruited from young men. Instead of regarding the whole diocese and each parish within it as a seed-bed – the meaning of *seminarium* – of vocations and preparing a flexible and long-term system of training for those who may be called to be ministers of the Church at any age, we have developed, so to speak, a greenhouse method of selection and training. This pattern needs a thorough overhaul.

This also means, of course, the ordination of married as well as of single men. Departure from the long-standing practice of ordaining only those who are called to celibacy has all the justification it needs in Scripture and cannot be claimed to be a misinterpretation of the will of Christ for his pastors. It arises naturally out of the need to conform ourselves to the reality of the Church as a single unified worshipping body, not a society making a sharp distinction between clergy and laity.

We should also reconsider the present policy of ordaining to the presbyterate immediately after completing their training those men who offer themselves for the pastoral ministry

A PEOPLE OF PRIESTS

when comparatively young. It would be better if they could have as their first aim the diaconate and then spend a number of years as deacons before being selected for presbyteral ordination. In the days when the presbyterate was almost entirely thought of as the granting of power to celebrate mass and hear confessions, it was generally considered that deacons had little or nothing to do in a parish. But now that the teaching and public service rôles of the ordained clergy are being brought out much more, it is clear that a deacon has a great deal to do in a parish by way of building up the community of faith and ensuring that the faith is translated into practice. Ordaining to the presbyterate a young man in his mid-twenties has the effect of reducing to the level of ritual a function – that of the headship of a worshipping community – that should best be entered into only at the time when it can be exercised in reality.

The threefold structure of the sacrament of Order makes it possible for us to adapt the system by appropriate stages. Experience gained from the selection, training and pastoral experience of married deacons, mature men whose knowledge of life and practice of the faith equip them for parish service, may indicate the feasibility of further changes. Men who have lived by the gospel, and have reflected and relied upon it while living their working and family life may well prove themselves true pastors of the Church in their mature years.

A Pastoral Spirituality

The spirituality commended in seminaries and urged upon priests since the Council of Trent has centred on the Eucharist: on the holiness required of the priest as a consequence of his identification with the sacrificial death of Christ on the Cross. There can be no quarrelling with that, as it is the cen-

BISHOPS, PRESBYTERS AND DEACONS

tral teaching of Christ himself that we must die to self to rise with him.

Since the Second Vatican Council, priests have been searching for a further principle on which to base their way of life and their prayer. To be sacrificed, yes; but to be sacrificed by doing what?

The argument of this book has been that the sacerdotal image does not bring out the specific calling of the ordained ministers and that to understand their contribution to the priestly worship of the Church other images have to be used, notably that of pastor. Their purpose in life must be to gather together and care for the People of God, his Church. In doing this, they are servants of the Word of God; the Word is the focus of their thought, the subject of their conversation, the language of their communion with others.

Ordination does not create 'ministers of Word and sacrament', as if the teaching and speaking part of our service could be distinguished from a ceremonial or ritual part, so that words and actions are set in separate categories. As servants of the Word, the apostles and their successors have one focus, not two: Christ who is the Word of God in his entire person, speaking and acting, words and deeds, all of a piece, eloquent in his slightest look and gesture, creative whenever he opens his mouth to speak.

Bishops, presbyters and deacons have a shared spirituality; they have to know and speak the language of the Word of God. Whatever the particular work assigned to them in the Church – teaching, healing, studying, administration – whatever their age, whether or not they belong to a particular religious family, with its particular inclination towards action or contemplation, the responsibility has been laid upon them of helping the People of God to live together according to the law of Christ, and to speak his word.

5

The Priests of the Parish

The deeper understanding of the mystery of the Church that has guided reform and renewal in the twentieth century finds practical expression above all in the life of the parish, the local community within which individual Christians live their lives and through which they are in communion with the Church of all the world. Well before the Second Vatican Council, efforts were already being made to lay a fresh emphasis on the all-embracing family life which the Church should provide in her parish communities, and which had been obscured by the rise of devotional and charitable groups catering for special interests. Individual personal devotion was fostered, but the sense of the Church as a community open and accessible to all and given full expression in every neighbourhood was diminished. The Church is the contemporary support and guide of our faith, existing not just in theory or as a world-wide society, but one that calls upon us to identify with the people amongst whom we live.

How does the understanding of the priesthood of Christ and of our priesthood that has been set out in the previous chapters affect the day-to-day life of this local expression of the Church? It is not enough just to think of ourselves in ways derived from the gospel, important as it is to use the right terminology and to grasp its meaning. The thoughts worked out in study and meditation must be expressed in practice. Those who are called to worship God in different

THE PRIESTS OF THE PARISH   119

ways as members of his People need to learn to fit in with one another, working together to build a community worthy of being called God's family. Without attempting to go into precise organizational detail, this chapter looks at the parish as an essential cell of Church life and at the character it should acquire in the light of its professed faith.

If the ordained minister, as 'the parish priest', is thought of in predominantly sacerdotal terms, emphasizing the ritual that he alone is allowed to perform, and the people he serves have very little notion of their own sacerdotal character, shared with him by virtue of their baptism and their faith, relationships are very different from those that can exist when all are aware of their common life in the one priestly Body of Christ. The Church is at present moving from an epoch when the former restricted view of priesthood predominated to one in which the images specifically applied in the New Testament to the People as a whole and to the ordained ministry within that People are being given their proper corporate expression, in which all members join together in the exercise of the one shared priesthood conferred upon them all by God.

A People on the Move

The name given to the local Christian community, 'parish', from the Greek *paroikia*, does not primarily denote a territorial area. Its main significance is that of a temporary dwelling place, particularly in a foreign land, and its application to the Church derives from the teaching of St Peter on the journeying life of God's People:

> Once you were not a people at all and now you are the People of God; once you were outside the mercy and now you have been given mercy. I urge you, my dear people,

while you are visitors and pilgrims [*paroikoi kai parepide-moi*] to keep yourselves free from the selfish passions that attack the soul. Always behave honourably among the pagans. (1 Pet. 2:10–12)

It tells us that the local church is on a pilgrimage; that they are a people on the move. Boundaries are necessary so that pastoral care can be properly shared out and organized; so the other familiar term 'diocese', used originally to denote a subdivision of the Roman Empire, is now applied to the area occupied by a local church under the pastoral care of a particular bishop, and parishes have their own allotted territories within the diocese.

But it is true of the whole local church, the diocese, called together and cared for by its bishop, as it is of each individual parish with its presbyters, deacons and other ministers, that they derive their identity not from the land they occupy but from the Person in whom they believe and with whom they are advancing towards their goal of individual and corporate fulfilment in heaven.

Paradoxically, Christ's followers think of themselves both as citizens and as strangers. In this world, they are at home, yet they are travellers; they are firmly based, yet always on the move. Membership of a parish means that they are known and recognized by others and enjoy stability and security; but it also involves them in living their lives as a journey along with all those who share their purpose and goal.

So the parish community is defined and held together simply by its shared faith. Other factors have their part to play: culture, language, nationality. But what makes the parish Christian is the one motive shared by all: the call of Christ to meet and to follow him together. Christ is found within his family. The public acknowledgement of that fact is the essential sign of faith. By being present at mass we are opening ourselves to the knowledge of Christ within the community

THE PRIESTS OF THE PARISH 121

that he intended should be our teacher, and at the same time are ourselves bearing witness to the world that surrounds the Church and is searching for its Saviour.

A People on the Move

Since the Christian life is lived in the parish, the place of pilgrimage, the rule of the Church, that we should join in her worship every Sunday, the day of the Resurrection, and on certain other feasts particularly expressive of our faith, is the simple key to the essential 'practice' of Christianity. Many other actions are important: praying, reading the Scriptures, visiting the sick, living in charity with our neighbours, helping the poor, keeping cheerful. You would not be a real Christian without them. But joining in worship with other members of the parish: that is the recognized sign of citizenship, the step towards the goal that gives our lives their meaning.

By starting the week in this way, we are conscious of continuing a pattern established at the beginning, and continuing ever since the Resurrection:

In the evening of that same day, the first day of the week, ... Jesus came and stood among them. (John 20:19)

Eight days later the disciples were in the house again ... Jesus came in and stood among them. (John 20:26)

We no longer see the Risen Christ, but he has given us enduring signs of his presence, signs which keep our personal pilgrimage moving along the right path. Discerning our way is not a lonely struggle; discovering that we are at one with others in recognizing Our Lord and in listening to him gives us confidence in answering the special call that comes to each one of us. There is a shared language that each one of us speaks in a personal and particular way, but that all understand.

The corporate nature of this pilgrimage is the consequence of the gift of the Christian faith itself, which involves both reconciliation and communication, never one without the other. Christ came to reconcile us to his heavenly Father and to one another, and communication is the result, communication with God, with our contemporaries in the Church, and from one generation to the next. Faith comes from hearing, and so must be spoken and shared in conversation, not just read about in private. When we meet together for worship, we believe him to be present among us, uniting us and relating us to one another.

The parish community gathers together all classes and all ages. Reconciliation takes place and bears fruit at all levels, individual, social, cultural and political; with the forgiveness of sins there comes the ending of quarrels and the making of peace. Social distinctions used to be much more obvious at the parish assembly. Today we are made less aware of them within the parish, but they are still operative, as a problem facing the movement for Church unity, for example; divisions have social causes as well as theological ones.

The presence of both young and old at mass in the parish makes continuity in time real in practice. The next generation is already here. A Church without young people has slipped out of the living movement of tradition, which receives the faith from the past in order to pass it on, increased and embellished in its expression, to the future.

The Church does of course provide for human variety in all its forms, so that everyone can feel at home. There are Knights of Malta as well as Knights of St Columba, Carthusians, withdrawn from the affairs of the world, as well as workers among the poor and deprived of every kind. In the parish itself there are organizations catering for diverse interests. But it is the link with the parish that is common to

THE PRIESTS OF THE PARISH

all of these, and a life lived without acknowledgement of the universal family in its local expression would not be a Christian life in its full dimension; if these groups acted in such a way as to reinforce class distinctions, stimulating jealousy and antagonism, they would be working against the purpose of the Church as God's means of making peace. They should all see themselves as making a distinctive contribution to the corporate life of the whole human family in its particular expression in a single neighbourhood, without which it would exist only as a theoretical ideal.

Meeting together in the parish for worship, in the one local assembly that is designed for all those who live together in one place, we discover also the extent of the concern for the human family, the universal invitation offered to all, that is expressed by the presence of Christ among us in our local society. This has a significance for our own life of faith. Finding Christ in the Church means that our minds and hearts are focussed not on our own private inner experience, but on a person separate from ourselves, to whom others are related as well. He is part of the external world and gives us our place in that same world.

Prayer is not the contemplation of ourselves or the search for some private benefit; it is that which takes us out of ourselves into an experience of the other, who is God, who made himself known at a particular time and place and among particular people and who makes himself visible in a different way, but a way just as real, in our own time and place. Christ engages our full personal response; because he is reliable and trustworthy, he seizes the whole of our attention, enabling us to forget ourselves, to 'die to self', in the gospel phrase, and therefore to grow, releasing the energies and talents that otherwise, lacking an aim beyond themselves, remain unused.

And this awareness and love of God is never separate from our awareness and love of others. Relating us to God, prayer relates us more closely to our fellow human beings. The

124   A PEOPLE OF PRIESTS

parish, the local expression of the universal Church, is its true setting and support.

Every Ordination Serves the Parish

Not all of those ordained to the diaconate, presbyterate or episcopate are directly involved in the service of a parish. Many are occupied in auxiliary work of one kind or another: in specialist studies, in administrative posts, in works of charity of all kinds. But it is the parish that makes sense of all this activity. These ordained ministers must think of themselves as contributing, in many different ways, to the overall purpose of the Church: the building-up of complete worshipping families of the Church, where people find themselves in relationships with others from birth to death, from baptism to its fulfilment.

Within the people of priests, in one way or another, there must be fishermen and pastors, contributing to the life of the people by calling them together, teaching them, confirming their faith and nourishing their life. Ordination is not a gift to the private devotion of the individual, crowning his baptismal priesthood with a kind of super-priesthood that gives him a status and a situation independently of any work he may undertake. Whatever the ordained minister does, he cannot think of himself as in some way working alongside the parish, still less above it, in the life of the Church. As part of the whole worshipping company of priests, his personal, ultimate responsibility is the service of the gospel in its most accessible day-to-day reality: the parish, the family that makes available in each locality the wider diocesan expression of the Catholic Church under the care of its pastor, the bishop.

The ordained ministers who are given the direct care of parishes are doing the work that is most characteristic of the mission and function of the Church. The ideas we have

THE PRIESTS OF THE PARISH 125

inherited that incline us to regard 'diocesan' or 'secular' priests as some sort of lesser breed of clergy by comparison with the members of religious orders are derived from particular cultures of the past, not from the original pattern given to the Church. Parishes must not be allowed to slip to the lowest place in the Church's priorities, but must always be understood as the places where the Church is most visible, with a membership drawn from all nations, classes and ages.

'Religious' are people who, within the manifold activity of the Church, have chosen a particular way of working out their salvation. As teachers, or nurses, or as people offering other forms of service, including the life of contemplation and prayer, they promote the life of the Church community. Some of them are given an overall pastoral role as bishop, presbyter or deacon that commissions them as leaders of the community as well as specialists making their own distinct contribution. Others are not ordained. If we are to enable the Church to work properly, with due understanding of her structure and purpose, we should always see them as ancillary to the parish. Without that orientation beyond themselves, without their contribution to the health of the whole organism in its local expression, they would be like leaven that has not been put into the bread. The ordained servants of the parish can come from any source, religious or not, married or celibate, in youth, middle age or old age. Any depreciation of their status, any suggestion that they are but the Church's infantry, tradesmen, routine agents, is a reversal of priorities due to human vanity, not a feature to be given lasting house-room in the life of the Church.

The pilgrimage theme provides the proper context for understanding the very specific and irreplaceable role of the ordained ministers in the Church, and their relationship to the life of the parish. It is sometimes said that this emphasis on the pastoral care for which they are to be held responsible creates a danger of making them into social workers who are concerned only with people's physical welfare and who forget their role as celebrants of the sacraments, the principal expressions of the Church's worship. But the sacraments are not properly celebrated unless they are set within their pastoral context and seen as indicating the meaning and direction that we need to discern within the circumstances of our pilgrimage.

The sacraments can neither be divorced from the life of Christ in which they enable us to share nor from the history of our individual lives. Interpreted outside the context provided by our faith – for example as guarantors of good luck or as a device for escaping the inexorable hand of fate – they lose their true meaning.

The pastors of the Church are helpers and guides on our pilgrimage, celebrating the sacraments that start us on our way and mark each stage of the journey, leading us back if we lose our direction. The mysteries that we celebrate are not magic spells or gestures born of superstition; if they are seen not as timeless gestures independent of any context, but as stages along a journey in which we are engaged, moments of choice in a joint enterprise between each one of us and God, the guiding role of the minister can be seen to demand understanding, wisdom and insight as he sets out to communicate the knowledge and light that God has provided.

Representing Christ: All Those Present

Although it is part of a people without limits or frontiers, the Catholic parish can be identified by various specific signs that mark it off from the gatherings of other denominations and other religions. This can appear to indicate a narrowness of outlook and concern; why should Christ be fully represented by only one of the churches in our particular district? In fact, the insistence on the identification of one group

THE PRIESTS OF THE PARISH   127

among many is inseparable from the purpose of the Church as the world-wide means of reconciliation. The peace which is offered to all is a really existing community of peace, at one with itself. The means given to bring about unity must itself be united. A Saviour whose message was only for a few and who left others outside their number to find their salvation elsewhere would not be an assured and certain Saviour. The Catholic people is clearly recognizable as his representative in each particular local expression of its life.

This possibility of identifying the Church in each parish arises out of the share given to each person present in the unique priesthood of Christ, who enables us to join together in worship. Each one of us has a different life, different gifts and activities to offer, as the result of Christ's call, given at baptism, to be part of his priestly, worshipping body; each one of us therefore represents him in a different way. This combination of unity in Christ and human diversity is one of the signs of the presence of the Catholic Church.

The technical phrase *in persona Christi* (in the person of Christ; representing Christ), applied in the documents of the Church and in theological writing to the action of the bishop or the presbyter whose particular task it is to preside at the Eucharist, has as its first and fundamental meaning this general sense, arising out of the membership of the Body of Christ that is shared by all the baptized. When they were ordained as bishop or presbyter, they did not cease to be baptized Christians who had already represented him to the world. Their primary awareness must be of the status that all worshippers have in common as disciples of Christ. Together with all others who offer the Eucharist, they offer themselves in loving obedience, seeking to bring themselves into harmony with the will of God, and asking to be made holy and so to be acceptable and authentic worshippers. They were part of the Good Shepherd's flock before they were given any special role in it, and that identity, shared with all other members, remains with them. Established in Christ, they are always part of his Body; Christ is his Body as much as he is its Head. To do justice to this reality, St Paul speaks of the whole gathered community, Head and members together, as 'Christ' (1 Cor. 12:12).

The phrase *in persona Christi* does indeed also apply to them in the special sense that derives from their ordination, when they carry out their pastoral mission of calling together the members of Christ's Church and providing them with the means by which they can truly worship Almighty God; but they must always bear in mind this fundamental sense, which constantly reminds them that they are not Christ's only representatives in the parish assembly.

This understanding of the phrase arises out of the fact that the Apostles were told that 'Anyone who welcomes one of these little children in my name, welcomes me; and anyone who welcomes me welcomes not me but the one who sent me' (Mark 9:36–7). In response to a question they had put to him that had betrayed their feelings of self-importance, as persons chosen to be responsible office-bearers in the Kingdom of Heaven, Christ told them that part of the message they had to deliver was that they were not his only representatives. Innumerable other people, including children, act *in persona Christi* to offer us salvation, in an incalculable number of ways.

To grasp the full sense of the expression, it must be taken in its general sense first of all. It even applies when we are unaware that the universal principle of Christ's communication with us is at work. One has only to recall the description of the Last Judgement to realize the countless ways in which Christ presents himself to us: ' "Lord, when did we see you hungry and feed you? . . . In so far as you did this to one of the least of these brothers of mine, you did it to me" ' (Matt. 25:37–40). Discipleship of Jesus need not be aware of itself, and the discovery of Jesus in others can occur

THE PRIESTS OF THE PARISH

without our realizing it; what is essential is that we should have responded to the opportunity of doing good when it was presented to us.

A positive conviction that one is a member of God's People can never be allowed to be accompanied by a reverse conviction that others do not stand for him. The deeper our own faith, the more we should be able to recognize and acknowledge the presence of faith in others, including the faith implied in every assent to the good impulses of grace. ' "No one who works a miracle *in my name* [my italics; Our Lord was declaring his recognition and acceptance of one whom John described as 'not one of us'] is likely to speak evil of me" ' (Mark 9:38–40).

The members of the Church have been gathered together from all sections of humanity; they are on that account a sign of Christ's presence to all other human beings, and so a means of their salvation: ' "If anyone gives you a cup of water to drink just because you belong to Christ, then I tell you solemnly, he will most certainly not lose his reward" ' (Mark 9:41).

Further to this, the strongest impression left by a reflection on the ways in which, according to the New Testament, Christ is present to our generation and to all others is his representation above all by the poor, to whom he brought the Good News. So the parish assembly must always bear in mind that in coming to hear the Word of God and to worship him they are equipping and strengthening themselves for service to the poor and the weak: the sick, the young, the old, the hungry, those suffering in every way in all parts of the world. That is what makes the Christian Church in her world-wide presence and expression the most powerful of all agents for change and human progress; truth to her own nature demands the unselfconscious and unself-righteous service of all others, in whom she sees Christ and by whom she knows herself to be judged.

Representing Christ: Bishops, Presbyters and Deacons

As members of the Church, set apart by their baptism to worship God in the priestly body of the Church, bishops, presbyters and deacons, each with their different range of responsibilities within the one shared sacrament of Order, have by that sacrament also been chosen and given authority to speak and act for Christ in a special and distinct sense: Christ the Head of the Church and Shepherd of his People has appointed them to gather his people together and lead them in worship. The phrase *in persona Christi* applies to them in this additional sense. To quote the Council's Dogmatic Constitution on the Church:

> The ministerial priest, by the sacred power he enjoys, moulds and rules the priestly people. Acting in the person of Christ (*in persona Christi*), he brings about the Eucharistic Sacrifice, and offers it to God in the name of all the people. (*L.G.* n. 10)

The Decree on the Ministry and Life of Presbyters put it this way:

> Since in their own measure presbyters share in the office of the apostles, God gives them the grace to be ministers of Christ Jesus among the people ... For, through the apostolic proclamation of the Gospel, the People of God is called together and assembled so that when all who belong to this People have been sanctified by the Holy Spirit, they can offer themselves as 'a sacrifice, living, holy, pleasing to God' (Rom. 12:1). Through the ministry of presbyters, the spiritual sacrifice of the faithful is made perfect in union with the sacrifice of Christ, the sole Mediator ... The ministry of presbyters is directed towards this work and is completed by it. (P.O. n. 2)

It is the Christ who called his Apostles together and gave

THE PRIESTS OF THE PARISH 131

them pastoral responsibility, who continues today to send his representatives among us. The bishop and the presbyter speak and act for him; because we believe in him and trust him, we receive their words and actions as from him, to be understood in the light of his teachings and of his Spirit.

Just as priesthood must be understood as characteristic of the whole People of God, so also *in persona Christi* must be seen as applying to everyone in different ways. Bishops, presbyters and deacons are not the only ones who stand *in persona Christi*; but they have their special way of representing him, on speaking and acting *in persona Christi*, which others do not have.

Through the sacrament of Holy Order, Christ gives his people the means of joining themselves to him so that they can become, with Christ, an acceptable offering, speaking with one voice in the praise of God. As the shepherds chosen and sent by him, the bishops, presbyters and deacons must provide for us the whole life of Christ in his teachings, in his gift of himself, and in his work each day as he makes us into worshippers with him. Their consecration and mission give them the responsibility of leading the People of God in the name of the head and of nourishing them, as Christ himself was nourished, with the knowledge of the will of God and the strength to obey it.

Their personal charge from God does not cut them off from the remainder of the priestly body, but identifies them more closely with them, just as Christ has identified himself with us and our needs. They speak for those they care for as shepherds in the name of Christ, and their first qualification to speak is the fact that they are part of the flock themselves. *In persona Christi* applies to them in two ways: as sharing in the Body and as caring for the Body, as members of Christ and as pastors for Christ. They must be aware of the problems and difficulties of those with whom they live, concerned for them in their prayer to God and in their work for the

132   A PEOPLE OF PRIESTS

society of which they are part; and they bring to those problems and difficulties the teaching, strength and grace provided
by Christ.

In the parish assembly we find a gathering having just the
same structure and embodying the same relationships and
forms of service and stewardship as established themselves
round Our Lord and his Apostles in the beginning. The
Conciliar Decree on the Liturgy brought this out by speaking
of the different ways in which Christ is present in the
worship of the Church: in the 'two or three' who are gathered
together, in the reading of the Scriptures, in the person of his
ministers, in his body and blood. We find him there in the
flock as well as in the pastor, in the persons who need and
seek his words as well as in the words themselves. We are
united with our fellow Christians at the same time as we
are joined with him: never one without the other.

The Real Presence: the Presence of Reality

Attendance at the Eucharist can be understood as a weekly
meeting with the people of the world as made and remade
by God. From our side, we come before God as members of
the human race. In the parish church, we can hope to find a
sample of the local community. Other gatherings are limited
in their scope: peoples, parties, families, friends, work, hob-
bies, recreation. This one has no human limits or restrictions,
but meets together in answer to God's universal call to live
at peace with one another. We are there not on a class or
private interest basis, but in response to the call of God,
acknowledging our equal need to take part, in view of our
failures, and our equal privilege to be present in virtue of
God's forgiveness and his making us fit to worship him.

And coming from God, the Real Presence of Christ
answers our needs and enables our worship. Christ is 'really

THE PRIESTS OF THE PARISH 133

present'; this familiar affirmation of our faith in the Eucharist can be turned the other way round, to remind us that we are in the presence of the One who is reality itself. We join in the Eucharist because we know our lives to be full of unreality: not just of failure to match up to the standards set by God, but of deceit, insincerity, hypocrisy. Hearing Christ, seeing him in others and their needs, receiving his gift of himself, we recognize reality and become a little less unreal ourselves.

We continually need to recall that our going to mass is moved by this Real Presence, which is external to ourselves. The law of the Church, that we are to be present at mass on the Lord's day, brings out the duty laid on us by God's invitation and takes away any idea that we are just following our own tastes, pursuing a personal interest, or even paying a compliment to our Creator. Human motivations will be present; but the fundamental reason is laid upon us from outside.

Our presence at mass is needed for our own health and our salvation. The parable of the wedding feast shows how insistent is God's invitation (Matt. 22:1–14). The words of Scripture that we read focus our minds on the most significant events and persons of our history. They relate us to the real life of people who by playing their part in the working-out of God's purpose have shown us the way to understanding and directing our own lives. It is already important that we should take our place among all those, rich and poor, old and young, who are our neighbours in the human race; it is still more important that we should, in that company, identify ourselves with those through whom God has made himself known to us in a particularly significant way.

The words of Scripture and the story they tell of God's dealings with humanity put us in touch with the world as he has made it and with human history as he has guided it. That is why the mass is our source of health. If we find ourselves out of tune with what we hear, if we would prefer to pick and choose according to our own limited desires, then we are in some way detached from the wholeness that Scripture contains. The Word of God, if we will listen, exposes the restrictions of sympathy, the refusals of opportunity, the hoarding of talents that prevent us from being ourselves and from being present in the real world around us.

Every mass has its own special theme, and its own special word for each individual person. That special theme and that special word both lead us to one and the same gesture of Christ, by which he sums up every other way he speaks to us and influences us: the giving of his Body and Blood. We must hear his teaching, we must know the events of his life, we must believe and affirm the faith of the Church that he has sent to teach us: all this in order to know who it is that gives himself to us today.

We believe Christ because his actions are all of a piece with his words. The self-giving, the concern for others, the love that his words teach us are made real for us by this most eloquent of signs: the body and blood that tell us the meaning of the Cross and make us part of the Risen Christ who conquered the death we sought to inflict upon him.

The reality that Christ makes present at every mass is the living demonstration of the truth of his saying that we must die to find life:

'I tell you, most solemnly,
unless a wheat grain falls on the ground and dies,
it remains only a single grain;
but if it dies,
it yields a rich harvest.' (John 12:24)

In the Eucharist, his obedience to his heavenly Father, his death, and the harvest of his Resurrection become effective and nourishing for us, confirming his teaching and bringing us together to hear it today.

THE PRIESTS OF THE PARISH 135

We say that Christ is the High Priest of every Eucharist because the central action of every Eucharist conveys his love of God and his love for us. His worship of the Father, his due service, is his work for our salvation: the gift of himself to us so that we may be changed. Filled with his love, we too have been made priests, each in our own way. We are able to be priests because we have been made whole; we can really worship because we have been made real.

One Priesthood, Many Ministries

> To move effectively towards creating a laity with a real voice and capacity for decision, nuns and monks must detach themselves from clerical attitudes. They must associate instead with those outside the sacristy, away from the altar and apart from formation-houses and retreat-houses with an exclusively clerical flavour. Otherwise they will continue to reproduce a clerical mentality and lifestyle.[1]

This recent statement in a missionary quarterly is quoted here as an indication of the distance we still have to travel before classifications and divisions inherited from the past have ceased to hinder the work of the Church. This is the party spirit that ever since the days of the Corinthians has defined itself over against other members of the Church. Chapter 2 reflected on the clergy/laity theme and on the persistent divisions betrayed by our vocabulary; here we remind ourselves that the parish is the place where such divisions must be overcome.

Clearly, if what goes on in the sacristy and at the altar – in the parish church, in fact – is to be regarded as foreign to promoting a people active in the service of God in their daily

---

[1] Felipe J. Conto IMC, in *Mission Outlook*, 23, Autumn 1991, 65.

136   A PEOPLE OF PRIESTS

lives, then something has gone wrong. If 'a clerical mentality and lifestyle' is to be avoided like the plague by nuns, monks and the laity, then the clergy will soon be left high, dry and ineffectual.

The remedy for a situation of this kind is not a contrary affirmation of clerical separateness, but a reminder of the inner unity of the Church and a fading-away of the superimposed divisions. Our priesthood unites us; and in a parish our united worship is offered in innumerable ways.

The sacrament of Order must be understood in the New Testament sense of being the appointed means of bringing about harmony and orderly relationships within the Church (Chapter 4, pp. 103–6). The ministry undertaken by those who receive and live that sacrament is directed to the whole Body of Christ in a particular place. It must be concerned with the lives of all the Christian people and all other people in the same area: with the whole of life, from the cradle to the grave, with education in the faith, with the care of marriages, with the consolation of the dying and the bereaved, with the living Christian character of the community, both private and public. Every bishop and presbyter has a ministry to the whole Body of Christ.

This ministry must be exercised among the people, because that is where Christ was sent and where he continues to send his apostles. It must be exercised in his name, and he is for all times and places, so it will have future generations as well as the present one in mind. It will not be the voice of one time or place, of one tongue, class or nation, but the voice of the Word of God.

Deacons, working together with the bishops and presbyters in the service of the same Word, will help to make sure that those who hold pastoral oversight do not lose touch with the practical needs of their people. In a parish, presbyters and deacons will constantly have in mind the proclamation of the Word of God to all those living in the territory and the

THE PRIESTS OF THE PARISH   137

community assigned to them. The practising members of their parish will be a principal means of communication with others.

The proper development of the ministry of Reader is going to be needed if this aspect of our celebrations is to become effective; all that has been said about 'serving the Word' in the preceding pages must have its expression in public worship, in which many voices are to be heard, all requiring education and training.

The religious orders and congregations of the Church would lose their sense of direction if they did not see themselves as oriented towards the life of the parish, in which a complete cell of the life of the Church is to be found. In one way or another, all those who are dedicated to the religious life are occupied in seeing that the Church will flourish in her local expression: a community representative of all humanity.

The same applies to specialists in scholarship or in teaching. The many other ministries to which people are called in the Church all relate in different ways to the building up of the parish community, as do the movements and societies of all kinds that meet different needs, material and spiritual. The loving worship of God that is Christian priesthood is inseparable from the love of our neighbours which is found in every living parish.

Ordination for Women?

A time when the theological understanding of the ordained ministry is itself the subject of intense scrutiny is hardly the moment for the Church to give a definitive answer to this question. Before it can be settled, we need to be clearer in our minds about the distinctive gift that ordination conveys.

Much of the argument against the ordination of women derives from a concentration on the sacerdotal image as primary in the definition of the ordained ministry. But it has been maintained in these pages that essential to the new relationship between God and ourselves inaugurated by the New Testament is the fact that priesthood (*sacerdotium*) is now available to all and communicated to all, so that other images must be used – the ones employed in the New Testament itself – if the ordained ministry is to be properly understood.

The argument drawn from symbolism, seeing the presiding minister of the Eucharist as an image of Christ, representing him dramatically and even visually, so that women would necessarily be excluded, depends upon a particular liturgical culture and cannot be decisive. The choice and the sending of the Apostles and their successors gives them ambassadorial status, within which they retain their individual and distinct character. They do not, so to speak, become ikons of Christ.

The enquiry into the admissibility of women to the ordained ministry must centre on determining the reasons why Christ chose only men to be his Apostles. This would include a study of the particular images he used to convey their responsibilities, which, as we have seen, denote for us the distinct character of their priesthood. This has hardly yet been done. Does some New Testament scholarship tend to treat Christ as a passive agent, not giving him enough credit for personal initiative and for knowing what he was doing?

It could be pointed out, for instance, that in giving the Apostles authority Christ was not affirming patriarchy, still less prelacy, but giving them a service role in his Kingdom.

This debate needs another book. The contribution made here must be limited to the attempt to show in what way bishops, presbyters and deacons are priests: not more priests than anyone else, but priests of a specific kind, exercising pastoral care.

Ecumenism and Ministry

Differences over the definition of ministry still keep Christians apart. The argument presented here, showing that the whole Church is priestly and that the special priesthood of bishops, presbyters and deacons is best understood in pastoral and other biblical terms, should remove Protestant fears of a sacerdotalism that obscures and restricts the extent of God's gift to us in Christ.

The search for reconciliation should concentrate on the ordained minister's role in relation to the authentic teaching of the gospel. The problem is not simply to determine who has the power to consecrate the Eucharist validly, but to whom has been given the pastoral oversight of the Church, which involves in the first place a commissioning to teach the whole message of the gospel and to commend it to our response in faith. The Eucharist is part of that 'whole message', confirming in action the words of Christ, and must always be seen in that setting. Authentic communion is communion in a single faith. We do not have to choose between a Christianity that has 'ministers of the Word' and another that has 'ministers of the Sacraments'. The ministry of the Word is complete when it culminates in sacramental reality.

To Sum Up

The whole Church is 'a people of priests'. The service of God which we offer consists of consecrated lives, lives made over to God so completely that death itself is understood as the way to life. Our priesthood is received at our baptism; the baptismal rite signifies our passage with Christ through his own death and resurrection, so that we are able to love God as he does, if we will act in terms of the new life we have received. This action is priestly because it is in itself the direct service of God; and it is also priestly because it is related to the world around us, the world that we have to bring to God. As priests, we have to consecrate everything we touch: our work, our families, those whom we meet, all have to be brought to God and made capable of carrying out their true role within his creation.

The ministerial priesthood is not superior to the priesthood of the whole Church, because it is part of it. The more faithfully the ordained ministers carry out their work for the Body of Christ, the more truly all can be priests. Most of those whom we meet in the Church speak to us of Christ by their own person, by their family relationships or their work; some speak to us of Christ by being bishops or presbyters or deacons. Through them, Christ guides and teaches his Church; through them, Christ gives us our daily bread, his body and blood offered for the remission of our sins; through them, he pardons and counsels us; through them, he gives us our commission to serve him in the world; through them, he serves his Church.

There is one priesthood: the priesthood of Christ and of all the faithful. When Christ chooses some within this priesthood to be priests of a special kind, to be bishop-priests, presbyter-priests and deacon-priests, he does so in order that his life of true worship may be brought to everyone. Ordained for the work of the Church, bishop, presbyter and deacon are priests of the New Law, ordained by Christ to lead us from lifeless observances into the service of the living God.

THE PRIESTS OF THE PARISH   141

Postscript: The Question of Anglican Orders

In 1896, Pope Leo XIII, in the Bull *Apostolicae Curae*, declared that Anglican ordinations were 'absolutely null and utterly void'; in other words, that they did not establish anyone ordained in the Anglican Church as a minister of the Church in the same sense as that intended by Catholic ordinations. Obviously, if all Anglican bishops, presbyters and deacons were by virtue of their ordination ministers of exactly the same kind as the bishops, presbyters and deacons of the Catholic Church, the reunion of the two bodies would be made easier than it appears to be at present.

The investigation that led to the Bull of Leo XIII concentrated on the function of the bishop or presbyter as sacrificing priest. It was held that the Church of England in the sixteenth century had explicitly rejected teaching about the eucharistic sacrifice to which the Catholic Church was wholly committed in its ordinary everyday teaching and practice, and that ordinations conducted in the Anglican Church could not therefore be regarded as valid.

Controversy since 1896 has centred on sixteenth-century eucharistic doctrine and on the intention of the Anglican Reformers to continue the life of the Church as traditionally received. Anglican apologists have claimed that statements directed against Catholic teaching and practice in, for example, the Thirty-nine Articles of the Church of England, were to be regarded as rejections of extreme and erroneous positions held by some Catholic writers; they were not intended to exclude the classic teaching of the Catholic centuries, which the Church of England has always wanted to retain.

Not all Anglicans would be satisfied with this presentation of the Articles; they would defend as truly Anglican an exclusion of elements of eucharistic teaching that had been traditionally accepted in the Catholic Church. And Catholic

142   A PEOPLE OF PRIESTS

scholars would for the most part agree with them, maintaining
that teachings essential to their faith, not extremist theories,
had been set aside.

The more developed understanding of Holy Orders that
starts from the fundamental commission to teach, enables us
to see this question from a different perspective. Concentration on the power to consecrate the Eucharist gave rise
to an individualistic attitude to ordination, which could be
envisaged apart from its proper place within the united community. Separated from the teaching activity of the Church,
the sacraments and the power to celebrate them could be
envisaged in a quasi-magical way.

The establishment of eucharistic communion and the joint
recognition of the ordinations carried out by separated
Churches is now seen to depend not just on a shared doctrine
of the Eucharist, but on a common understanding of the way
in which the entire revelation of God has been communicated,
and is still being communicated, absorbed and practised.

In addition to this, the Second Vatican Council made it
clear that the Catholic Church recognizes the working of
grace in the ministry and life of all Christian Churches and
communities (Decree on Ecumenism, *Unitatis Redintegratio*,
n. 3). The reconciliation of ministries will bring about completion and enrichment for all concerned.

This is conveyed in a text composed by the Congregation
for Divine Worship and the Discipline of the Sacraments for
use in the ordination of former Anglican clergy (v. *The Tablet*,
30 April 1994, 542):

> N [Candidate's name], the Holy Catholic Church recognises
> that not a few of the sacred actions of the Christian religion
> as carried out in communities separated from her can truly
> engender a life of grace and can rightly be described as
> providing access to the community of salvation. And so we
> now pray. (A period of silent prayer now follows.)

THE PRIESTS OF THE PARISH

Almighty Father, we give you thanks for the X years of faithful ministry of your servant N., in the Anglican Communion (or: in the Church of England), whose fruitfulness for salvation has been derived from the very fullness of grace and truth entrusted to the Catholic Church.

As your servant has been received into full communion and now seeks to be ordained to the presbyterate in the Catholic Church, we beseech you to bring to fruition that for which we pray. Through Jesus Christ, our Lord.

Amen.

Suggested Reading

Bernier, Paul, *Ministry in the Church*. A Historical and Pastoral Approach. Mystic, Connecticut, 1992.

An informative guide to the development of theology and practice from the beginning to the present day, suggesting future possibilities.

Collins, John N., *Diakonia*. Re-interpreting the Ancient Sources. New York and Oxford, 1990.

A study of the use of the term in both pagan and Christian literature which corrects much contemporary thinking: an indispensable contribution to the present debate about ministry.

Colson, J., *Ministre de Jésus-Christ ou Le Sacerdoce de l'Evangile*. Etude sur la Condition Sacerdotale des Ministres Chrétiens dans l'Eglise Primitive. Paris, 1966.

An enquiry into the biblical and immediately post-biblical Christian literature which brings out the originality of the New Testament dispensation under which ministers, as the instruments of Christ, carry out their priestly service by building up a holy people, a people of priests.

Culbertson, P. L. and Shippee, A. B. (eds.), *The Pastor*. Readings from the Patristic Period. Minneapolis, 1990.

A selection of writings on pastoral care from Ignatius of Antioch to Gregory the Great, and from the Council of Elvira (c. 300) to the Council of Chalcedon (451), with a commentary both practical and wise. 'Being a pastor is often a thankless job, surrounded by competitive peers while struggling to do ministry among a rebellious and rejecting laity' (16).

Donovan, Daniel, *What are they saying about the ministerial priesthood?*

SUGGESTED READING

New York, 1992.

A survey of the work of leading theologians since Vatican II, carefully attentive to the variety of opinion and emphasis.

——, *Episcopal Ministry*. The Report of the Archbishop's Group on the Episcopate. London, 1990.

This Anglican report, published by Church House, will be of service in the consideration of a number of pastoral and ecumenical issues besides the one under particular examination, the ordination of women to the episcopate. More thought is needed on the corporate or collegial exercise of the bishops' teaching mission.

——, *Etudes sur le Sacrement de l'Ordre*. Paris, 1957. ET: Collegeville, Minnesota, 1962.

An influential volume of essays which retains its importance for post-conciliar debates.

Faivre, Alexandre, *The Emergence of the Laity in the Early Church*. New York, 1990.

Faivre shows how, in the first two centuries, 'all Christians represented God's *kleros* . . . The various functions that existed in the Church could not be called "lay" rather than "clerical" or "clerical" rather than "lay" ' (211). From the third century onwards, a differentiation set in. In the present-day search for an understanding of the clergy-laity relationship, he does not propose any *simpliste* solution (a 'return to the past'), but makes us aware of the factors to be considered and the options open to us.

See also his *Ordonner la Fraternité*, Paris, 1992, a collection of studies in the practice of the early church that questions and renews contemporary thinking.

Hall, D. J., *The Steward*. A Biblical Symbol Come of Age. New York, 1982, revised edition, 1990. Study Guides available.

A work of exegesis that has been widely influential in all denominations in North America. 'The Christian view of stewardship starts with the stewardship of the One who did not grasp at equality with God, but was obedient (Phil. 2)' (44). 'In the most provocative and even exciting ways, the stewardship metaphor can revive and preserve what is most precious and indispensable in the concept of priesthood' (240).

Lécuyer, J., *Le Sacerdoce dans le Mystère du Christ*. Paris, 1957.

The priesthood of Christ, of the faithful, of the Apostles and of their successors.

Legrand, Hervé OP, '*Traditio Perpetuo Servata*? The Non-Ordination of Women: Tradition or Simply Historical Fact?', *Worship*, 1991, 6, 482–508; also in *One in Christ*, 1993, 1, 1–23. The French original was published in *Rituels: Mélanges offerts au Père Gy* OP, (Cerf, Paris, 1990).

An examination of the *status quaestionis*.

Manning, Cardinal H. E., *The Pastoral Office*, London, 1883.

'It is easy to deceive ourselves, but may we not reasonably believe that the next time the Church meets in Council, whether by the reassembling of the Council of the Vatican, or in any other way, the first duty will be to take up the work already prepared, and to define the Divine powers of the Episcopate, and its relation to its Head?' (218). Cardinal Manning's concern that bishops and priests should be aware of their obligation to perfection in carrying out their mission persuaded him of the urgency of that 'unfinished business', the definition of the divine institution of the episcopate, that was to be completed by Vatican II. He saw the pastoral office above all in terms of government, authority to rule.

——, *The Eternal Priesthood*.

'The priesthood ... is the state of perfection instituted by our Divine Lord to be the light of the world, and the salt of the earth' (38). The Cardinal's high demands are matched by a searching awareness of human weakness.

Martelet, G., *Deux Mille Ans d'Eglise en Question*. Paris, I, 1984, II and III, 1990.

In the conviction that the crisis of the priesthood is a crisis of the faith itself, Martelet has provided the fruits of an enquiry into the Church's understanding of her ministry, and thus of her mission in the world, from the beginning to the present day. While hoping for an English translation, one hopes also for a shorter work presenting his diagnosis and remedy to a wide public. Suffice it here to quote his Epilogue: 'Shepherd: the word sums up the whole truth for all Christians about the apostolic ministry of the Church' (III, 329).

Martin, Dale B., *Slavery as Salvation*. The Metaphor of Slavery in Pauline Christianity. New Haven and London, 1990.

SUGGESTED READING 147

'How do we explain the positive, soteriological use of slavery as a symbol for the Christian's relationship to God or Christ?' (xiv) 'Paul's slavery to Christ did not connote humility but rather established his authority as Christ's agent and spokesperson' (147).

Masure, Eugène, *The Diocesan Priest*. A Study in the Theology and Spirituality of the Priesthood. London, 1957.

A translation of his *Prêtres Diocesains*, which was itself an enlarged edition of an earlier work, *L'Eminente Dignité du Sacerdoce Diocésain*, a classic commendation of the vocation and status of 'seminary priests' through a study of the theology of priesthood.

Nichols, Aidan, *Holy Order*. The Apostolic Ministry from the New Testament to the Second Vatican Council. (Oscott Series, 5.) Dublin, 1990.

A manageable, stimulating and richly documented historical survey.

O'Connell, Hugh, *Education in Wisdom*. A Study in the New Testament Theology of the Pastoral Ministry. Rome, 1969.

'The first and most important function for which the pastor is prepared by meditation on the Scriptures is *didascalia* – teaching. In this the pastor continues the work of the Lord who "went about all Galilee, teaching in their synagogues, and preaching the gospel of the kingdom".'

Osborne, Kenan B., *Priesthood*. A History of the Ordained Ministry in the Roman Catholic Church. New York, 1988.

An account which asks questions, making possible an informed reflection on the problems involved both in the interpretation of texts and in contructing a theoretical basis for future practice.

Richards, Michael, 'Servants of the Word, Shepherds of the People', *The Clergy Review*, 1979, LXIV, 239–246.

The Ordained Ministry after Trent and after Vatican II. For this and other articles on Ministry, see also *The Church 2001*, 1982, 136–209.

Riesenfeld, Harald, 'The Ministry in the New Testament', in Fridrichsen, Anton, and others, *The Root of the Vine*, 1953, 96–127.

'Christ's ministry is a shared ministry' (113). Riesenfeld's study brings out the 'evident continuity between the time of Christ's first sending out of his disciples and the activities of the various officers after Easter and Pentecost'. 'Continuity is clear from the fact that the ministers fill the same functions in the Church that Christ ministerially performed during his life on earth' (122).

Vanhoye, A., *Prêtre Anciens, Prêtre Nouveau selon le Nouveau Testament*. Paris, 1980.

The new, unique, priesthood of Christ and of his priestly people.